0604865

MW00477760

ON LINE

WITHDRAWN

Life on the Shoulder

Rediscovery and Inspiration along the Lewis and Clark Trail

Gordon T. Ward

Lucky Press

Published by Lucky Press, LLC
126 South Maple Street
Lancaster, OH 43130
www.luckypress.com

ISBN-10: 0-9760576-9-7
ISBN-13: 978-0-9760576-9-7

Book design: Janice M. Phelps

PRINTED IN THE UNITED STATES OF AMERICA

Library of Congress Cataloging-in-Publication Data
Ward, Gordon T.
  Life on the shoulder : rediscovery and inspiration along the Lewis and Clark Trail / Gordon T. Ward.
      p. cm.
  ISBN 0-9760576-9-7 (trade pbk. : alk. paper)
  1. Lewis and Clark National Historic Trail--Description and travel. 2. West (U.S.)--Description and travel. 3. Ward, Gordon T.--Travel--West (U.S.) 4. Ward, Gordon T.--Diaries. 5. Spirituality. 6. Travel--Religious aspects. 7. Lewis and Clark Expedition (1804-1806) 8. Lewis, Meriwether, 1774-1809--Diaries. 9. Clark, William, 1770-1838--Diaries. I. Title.
F592.7.W36 2005
917.804'2--dc22

2005017046

CONTENTS

ACKNOWLEDGMENTS AND THANKS

My entire family, Todd and Susie Paige, Robert Boye, Louis Starr, Dayton Duncan, the Forbes family, the Wickline Family, the Kaufman family, Sandy Stuart, Jayne Geiger Wyatt, Joshua Balling, Priscilla Miller, New Jersey Network, the Diana family, Qualex, Inc., Chris Todd, Xercise, Communications Services, the Amery family, Slumberjack, Inc., the Drysdale family, Chester Camera, the Bradbury family, Rich Pipeling, the Bonelli family, Missouri Historical Society, Dan Todd, Pocono Produce, The Ernst Financial Group, King's Supermarket, Magna Group, Inc., Sealed Air Corporation, The Sports People, Mountain Sports, Far Hills Country Day School community, colleagues and friends and all of the countless, individual volunteers, supporters and sponsors of this journey

MAP OF THE JOURNEY

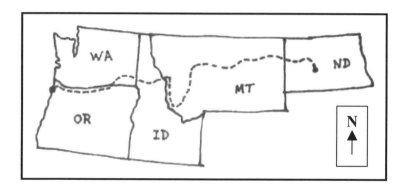

A SHORT NOTE ON THE HISTORICAL QUOTES
FROM THE LEWIS AND CLARK JOURNALS

Journal quotes from the original Lewis and Clark expedition have been inserted into some of my journal entries sections. These were added after *Life on the Shoulder* was compiled and arranged for the purpose of comparing the experiences that Todd and I had in 1994 with those of Lewis and Clark. While you will notice that several of the historical journal quotes are out of calendar order and may not coincide with the same locations described in my journal entries, the intention is to demonstrate that similar emotions and experiences were common to both trips. In addition, some of the historical journal quotes point out some dramatic changes that have occurred along the Lewis and Clark Trail since 1804. All of the original spelling, grammatical and punctuation errors have been preserved in these quotes.

FOREWORD

At the dawn of the nineteenth century, Lewis and Clark preserved the thoughts and experiences of their exploration in journals which are still read and enjoyed today as among this country's first written descriptions of the land west of the Mississippi. In keeping with this tradition, *Life on the Shoulder* is preserved and presented in its original, journal format, as a modern record of a journey completed in the very footsteps of the rugged Corps of Discovery. This approach has allowed me to best capture the flavor of the trip, and I feel it also serves as one of the few common bonds between the two expeditions, albeit one hundred and ninety years apart.

Life on the Shoulder is about a journey on many levels. It is one that travels back through time, experiencing the places known and recorded in the pages of history and the journals of Meriwether Lewis and William Clark. It is also a journey through the current American West, an area of diverse environments, staggering beauty and powerful natural forces. This is what I expected when I began this trip with my good friend Todd Paige in June of 1994. This is what we had worked and planned so hard to create, but this trip was to become much more. The landscape through which we traveled also proved to be one of emotional hills and valleys, mountains of elation, pits of exhaustion, prairies of boredom, storms of fear, anger and frustration, and stunning sun flashes of inspiration. It was a discovery of self and my connection with everything outside of my being. The spiritual lessons taught on this journey made me understand how narrow our scope of life can be, how much energy is wasted on worry, and how, at the moment when we feel we are most alone, we are truly in the company of our most trusted and dependable guides. While Lewis and Clark have been credited with exploring the western wilderness, I believe the exploration of the greatest wilderness lies just beneath the skin in the hearts and minds of us all.

I am finding that I continue to learn from the experiences of the trip to this day. As a result, I often look back and pinpoint moments on the journey when I was impressed with a better understanding of the events in my life, my expectations and their congruencies. A great deal of our time was spent literally riding "on the shoulder" of many roads and passing many sights while we in turn were passed by many other travelers, be they in cars, trains or logging trucks. It was unbelievably exciting, yet it also provided many opportunities for observation and reflection. The analogy to life became quickly apparent and led to the title of this book.

By living a "life on the shoulder," one allows oneself to step back and permit life's events to unfold naturally, at their own pace, with acceptance and without force. In doing so, by trusting the natural order, one is given the opportunity to realize, with a clearer understanding, the connections and interrelationships that exist between and among all things. With this comes a very profound sense of freedom, purpose and equality.

As an experiential education specialist, I welcome and value the power of direct experience. While personal growth is a continuous process, this trip brought to the fore, challenged, dashed and tested many of the beliefs that I had learned or had developed. The entire experience was a sort of spiritual litmus test for me. You will notice that the journal accounts contain philosophical and spiritual entries from time to time. These passages appear at points where I found fodder for thought and spiritual or philosophical affirmation. It is fulfilling to realize that the more I analyze the experience, the more I can gain in understanding.

Our journey was dubbed "Quest West," and its original purpose was to raise funds for a school scholarship at Far Hills Country Day School in New Jersey where Todd and I taught. Inspired by our friend Mr. Louis Starr, we selected the Lewis and Clark Trail because of his personal association with William Clark's personal diaries. Mr. Starr inherited the documents after they were discovered in December of 1952 in a rolltop desk that belonged to his grandfather. After Mr. Starr's lengthy and successful legal battle with the national government over possession rights, it was arranged for the papers to go to the Beineke Library at Yale University where they remain to this day.

Based on our passion for experiential education and the outdoors, Todd and I planned to cycle, backpack and canoe an 1,800-mile section of the trail, a conglomerate ribbon of modern highways, gravel roads, wild and scenic rivers and mountain trails, from Bismarck, North Dakota to Cannon Beach, Oregon. Our preparation was multifaceted and included intense physical training, tedious route planning and the establishment of contacts along the trail to name a few. Many thanks go out to the 1994 FHCDS Board of Trustees, Jayne Geiger Wyatt, FHCDS administration, faculty, parents, students, and all the sponsors of our trip. Special thanks are due to Priscilla Miller, our dedicated trip coordinator, and our own families for supporting and tolerating Todd and me in our preparation and travels. I am continually amazed at how well we all coexisted on our trip.

Since Todd was a math teacher and I taught history, we took advantage of every opportunity to include our trip into our classes during the year before we left. In fact, every department in the school got into the act. The Lewis and Clark expedition dealt with many areas of study including anthropology, biology, astronomy, geography, journaling and cartography, so it was relatively easy for classes to find different facets of the historical expedition on which to focus. Math classes even got involved with studies of bicycle frame design, angles and gear ratios.

When it came time for us to leave, we felt we were more than ready. We had communicated with state senators, park rangers, the media, historians and police, among others, and had done our homework in carefully plotting our itinerary. The plan called for Nini and Kate Diana, FHCDS alumni, to drive our support vehicle out to Bismarck, North Dakota where we would meet them. Todd and I would fly to St. Louis, Missouri in order to spend some time where Lewis and Clark began their journey in 1804. From there we would fly to St. Paul, meet my father in law Bob Boye, take a connecting flight to Bismarck where we would rendezvous with our support vehicle, which carried all of our gear, and begin our journey by cycling. Bob offered to drive our support vehicle, a recreational vehicle that came to be known affectionately as "the Rig," and join us on the three day canoeing section of our trip on the Wild and Scenic section of the Missouri River. When we got to Missoula,

Montana, Bob would fly home, and Todd's wife Susie would join us for the backpacking section over the Lolo Trail from Montana into Idaho. At the conclusion of the backpacking section, my then seven-year-old daughter Melina and her mom Kris would fly into Missoula, pick up the Rig and meet us in Idaho. Kris, Melina and Susie would then drive the Rig, as Todd and I completed our journey to the Pacific Ocean, once again on our bikes. And so it was that we began our journey.

Bedminster, NJ, 2005
Gordon T. Ward

Part 1

Saint Louis

An Invitation to the Moon

I want to drink in silver threads of moonlight
Captured and bottled –
Reflected off the face of the moon.
I wonder if I should save some for you,
Our spinning satellite,
Whose task it is to soar in circles
Endlessly
Unselfishly giving
All it catches
Back to us.
Pull up a chair and rest awhile.
I wish to make a wish
Come true for you.
Insanity you say?
Lunacy? Perhaps.
But sane men make

Their own madness.
Ignoring possibilities,
Lack of vision,
To never ask "What if?"
Is slow but certain
Cerebral suicide.
So let us break the mold, my friend.
Tear down the gates between our worlds,
Take the chance, run the risk.
Teach me to speak in tongues unfamiliar to this
*   world,*
And I shall offer you a draught so cool and sweet,
The likes of which you gave but never dared to
*   drink.*

Gordon Thomas Ward, September, 1992

Washington July 2nd 1803.
Dear Mother.

The day after tomorrow I shall set out for the Western Country; I had calculated on the pleasure of visiting you before my departure but circumstances have rendered this impossible; my absence will probably be equal to fifteen or eighteen months; the nature of this expedition is by no means dangerous, my rout will be altogether through tribes of Indians who are perfectly friendly to the United States, therefore consider the chances of life just as much in my favor on this trip as I should concieve them were I to remain at home for the same length of time; the charge of this expedition is honorable to myself, as it is important to my Country. For it's fatiegues I feel myself perfectly prepared, nor do I doubt my health and strength of constitution to bear me through it; I go with the most perfect preconviction in my own mind of returning safe and hope therefore that you will not suffer yourself to indulge any anxiety for my safety. . . .

You will find thirty dollars inclosed which I wish you to give to Sister Anderson my love to her Edmund & the family; Reuben writes me that Sister Anderson has another son; remember me to Mary and Jack and tell them I hope the progress they will make in their studies will be equal to my wishes and that of their other friends. I shall write you again on my arrival at Pittsburgh. Adieu and believe me your affectionate Son,
Meriwether Lewis

CLARKSVILLE 17TH JULY 1803

     . . . *I will cheerfully join you in an "official character" . . . and partake of the Dangers Difficulties & fatigues, and I anticipate the honors & rewards. . . . should we be successful in accomplishing it This is an immense undertaking fraited with numerous Dificulties, but my friend I can assure you that no man lives with whom I would prefer to undertake and share the Dificulties of such a trip than as yourself. . . .*

With every assurance of sincerity in every respect, and with affn. yr. fd. & H. Srv.

W. C. [William Clark]

PITTSBURGH AUGUST 3RD 1803.

Dear Clark:

. . . be assured I feel myself much gratifyed with your decision; for I could neither hope, wish, or expect from a union with any man on earth, more perfect support or further aid in the discharge of the several duties of my mission, than that, which I am confident I shall derive from being associated with yourself. . . .

Your sincere friend & Obt. Servt.

[Meriwether Lewis}

June 20, 1994 – Monday

Todd Paige and I began our journey today. My alarm sounded at 6:30 A.M. to usher into reality a dream that has been developing for eighteen months. There has been much planning, preparation and training, and we are eager and ready to go. It was especially difficult saying good-bye to Melina this morning, but I know that we will have a wonderful time when we meet in Idaho. Our plane left at 9:15 A.M. (forty-five minutes late), and we spent the next four hours traveling from Newark, NJ to Dayton, OH (arriving at 10:37 and lifting off at 11:15) and finally on to St. Louis, MO, arriving here at 11:10 A.M. Our flight was smooth but boring and included one time change. I get very anxious sitting in one place for long periods of time, so I looked forward to deplaning.

The area surrounding St. Louis where we stopped en route to North Dakota is extremely flat and not at all like northwestern New Jersey. We were happy to get our red rental car, especially since Todd and I had joked about driving a sporty, red car. Our destination in St. Louis, and our home base, is with Scott and Kathy Kaufman and their two daughters, Elizabeth (13) and Jennifer (18). They are a very warm and friendly family and make Todd and me feel very much at home and comfortable. We generally got to know each other through some wonderful conversations, some of which concerned the Wicklines, a family that we all know in New Jersey and our contact with the Kaufmans.

Later, at about 4:00 P.M., Todd and I visited William Clark's grave in Bellefontaine Cemetery, a fitting place to begin our journey. It was awe inspiring viewing the bust and monument. On the front of the bust is inscribed: "William Clark, born in Virginia, August 1, 1770. Entered into life eternal, September 1, 1838. Soldier, explorer, statesman and patriot. His life is written in the history of this country." Moving over to the right-hand side of the monument, it reads: "William Clark received his commission as lieutenant from George Washington in 1791. He was appointed Brigadier General by Thomas Jefferson in 1807, and reappointed as such by James Madison in 1811. He was made Governor of Missouri Territory by this president in 1813 and recommissioned twice by him. Being again appointed governor by James Monroe in 1820 who also made him superintendent of Indian affairs in 1822. His great fame as an explorer was won on the expedition of 1804, 5 and 6." Moving over to the left-hand side of the monument one can read: "This monument is erected with honor and loving memory of William Clark by his son, Jefferson Kearny Clark." On the back is a

Gordon (L) and Todd (R) at William Clark's Grave

quote in Greek from Deuteronomy I:21. It reads: "Behold, the Lord thy God hath set the land before thee. Go up and possess it."

On the inside of the two outer platforms flanking the monument are two inscriptions. The right-hand platform displays a wolf's head on the front, and on the rear one finds a head of a buffalo. This inscription says: " The expedition of Lewis and Clark across the continent in 1804, 5, 6 marked the beginning of the process of exploration and colonization which thrust our national boundaries to the Pacific." The left-hand platform has an opposite configuration. You find a buffalo on the front and a wolf on the back, and its inscription continues from the platform on the right by saying: "This primary exploration through more than four thousand miles of savage wilderness planted the flag of the United States for the first time on the shores of the Pacific Ocean. This completed the extension of the United States across the vast western region of the American continent and gave us our outlook toward the Orient."

Surrounding the grave, and of particular interest to us, are the graves of his sons, their wives and their children, but most notable, at least from my perspective, is something we found in the back of the circular plot, which is about thirty-four paces in diameter. Here there are two graves. One stone reads, "Louis Wilson, a faithful retainer of the family," and on another stone to the right is inscribed, "Emilene Payne, a good and faithful servant." These people were obviously servants, or maybe slaves of the family, but, in any case, it reflects the time period's not uncommon practice of including servants inside the family plot, which I thought was very interesting.

It was kind of eerie, looking at the bust in the gathering thunderstorm, and we were glad we went. There was no rain, but the thunder added to the overall ambiance and aura that surrounds the site; it made it even more intense and powerful. I noticed that the sight line of the bust of William Clark at one time had a direct view, now blocked by trees, out over the edge of the cemetery, which sits on a hill and overlooks the Missouri River and the point of departure for the Lewis and Clark expedition. This is an interesting connection that I'm sure was no accident. It certainly put things in perspective and highlights the magnitude of the original journey. This visit was most memorable, and we felt as if we had been in William Clark's presence as we departed, his bust staring out into the ominous approaching storm.

This evening we had an excellent dinner of beef brisket, fruit, and potato salad with the Kaufmans. Todd and I played pool after dinner. We placed calls to our homes and Dayton Duncan who had helped us with our preparation. It was good to hear Melina was doing well with me being gone. Dayton was excited for us and wished us the best of luck. Tomorrow will bring a reception at the Missouri Historical Society Building. Right now we're very tired and need to get our rest. The weather was hot (93°) and humid today. I hope tomorrow's weather will be better.

JUNE 21, 1994 – TUESDAY

We woke up to another hot and humid day (97°). After calling FHCDS and attempting to call other media contacts, we set out at 10:15 A.M. for the Jefferson Memorial Building and our 11:00 A.M. reception. Others in attendance were the Bonelli family (our friends from New Jersey), Dr. Archibald, Don Gallup and Karen Goering from the Missouri Historical Society and three local businessmen including Tom Andes from Magna Bank. During the reception, we were shown an original journal, bound in leather, that belonged to William Clark and was written during the expedition. I can't tell you how riveting it was to page through this original journal, look at maps and read words and information that was penned in Clark's own hand.

William Clark's original journal

After the reception, we all traveled to the Magna Bank corporate office building and sat for a formal lunch in a windowed room on the third floor that looked out east toward the St. Louis arch. We conversed about our trip, and it was exciting to discuss it with our hosts, a group of businessmen that were genuinely interested and impressed with our plans. Our lunch consisted of chicken with mushroom sauce and a great dessert of ice cream sundaes, items that will not be on our journey's munu. After lunch was finished, we were presented with checks for the Quest West Scholarship. Todd and I also each received generous gifts of a pen, money clip and a glass box.

Lunch was over at 2:00 P.M., so, later in the afternoon, Todd and I went to the St. Louis waterfront to do a little sightseeing. We went up the St. Louis arch and strolled around town which included a visit to the old courthouse where the Dred Scott case occurred.

After the thirty-minute trip home to the Kaufmans, we had a dinner of chicken, fruit, and potato salad. Elizabeth insisted on cutting fruit for us in order to make fruit salad because she guessed that this would be hard to come by on the trail. The Kaufman family is the best! We feel like members of the family. Postcards were written this evening after dinner. Unfortunately, Scott has been delayed and will be home late. It would be nice to meet him, but I don't think we will have the chance. A funny thing happened before I went to bed. Sugar, the Kaufman's dog, went into my pack, dragged out my jeans, pulled a pack of gum out of my pocket and devoured the entire pack leaving all of the wrappers on the floor. She's got an amazing nose! Tomorrow we are off to Bismarck, and Todd and I are anxious to go. We plan to leave at 9:30 A.M.

WILLIAM CLARK – MONDAY MAY 14TH 1804
  . . . *I Set out at 4 oClock P.M., in the presence of many of the neighboring inhabitants, and proceeded on under a jentle brease up the Missourie.* . . .

Part 2

North Dakota and Eastern Montana

JUNE 22, 1994 – WEDNESDAY

This marks the beginning of a more philosophical approach to these entries. Facts serve their purpose, and certainly will be included, but it is the emotion and spirit of the trip that will receive additional attention.

With much anticipation Todd and I left the Kaufmans today. We gave them two Quest West shirts on our departure. I could hardly sit still in the car and was not looking forward to the plane flight at all. I needed exercise. When we arrived at the airport, we found that our 11:55 A.M. flight from St. Louis to Minneapolis/St. Paul was canceled. It seemed that good karma was with us, however, because we got booked through standby on a TWA flight. The flight was supposed to take off at 11:55 A.M., but we didn't leave until 12:34 P.M. Luckily we arrived in Minneapolis/St. Paul at 1:49 P.M., just in time to meet Bob, get to the next gate in a half-hour and switch planes for Bismarck. We made it on board by 2:15, took off from Minneapolis/St. Paul at 2:33 and landed in Bismarck at 3:35 P.M. By 4:14 we were getting our baggage and thinking about our ride up to the KOA Campground. Whew!

Nini and Kate met us at the Bismarck airport right on time, and we arrived at the Bismarck KOA campground after adjusting the muffler pipe on the RV and shopping for food. Our bikes are packed and loaded. I can foresee that hot weather will be a concern, and we will be careful to drink plenty of fluid. Driving the RV, which has been dubbed the "Rig" by Todd, is not as difficult as it may seem by looking at it. It is sluggish, but it goes.

I feel as if we are all in a state of limbo where we are not sure how to act and what to say to each other. Perhaps it is the anticipation of the trip, which starts in earnest tomorrow. This is, for me, a very personal journey. It is in an area of the country that holds so much appeal for me and incorporates so much of our country's history. We had wondered what lay in wait for us as we gazed out across the wide, flat plains from the jet as we landed. Exhilaration, fear, worry and pride will be felt during our journey. This may be the reason for my self-consciousness. I am so focused on my inner self, my emotional preparation, that I find it difficult to deal with external information when it requires interaction and/or response. I believe this will begin to pass as we get a day or two of successful travel under our belts. Success will breed confidence and allow me to relax. This has been a long time in the planning stage, and I want it to go well.

JUNE 23, 1994 – THURSDAY

This was a full and varied day indeed. We pulled out of the KOA Campground at about five minutes to eight in the morning, and went to Bismarck for a repair. Our RV needed a cover replaced on the refrigerator vent, which is located up on the roof. Apparently it blew off on the trip out here. We got out of the RV repair shop in Bismarck at 9:08 A.M. and headed for Washburn, ND and Fort Mandan. We did however have the chance to call Joshua Balling, a reporter from the *Hills-Bedminster Press* in New Jersey, get in contact with a newspaper up in New Town, North Dakota, and tentatively set up a time to talk to them tomorrow. So, that's how we began. It was a bright, sunny day, not too hot, and we were looking forward to a good beginning ride today.

On the way to Fort Mandan we stopped in Washburn to ask directions. After talking to two people in the post office, they suggested that Todd and I tell our story to the local newspaper that was about seventy-five yards down the street. Joe, the editor, who incidentally was from Hightstown, NJ, took a real interest in our trip and promised to do a story in this week's paper. Across the street from the paper was an artist by the name of Bill Reynolds who was painting a large, detailed mural of Lewis and Clark at Fort Mandan on the wall of the Washburn Historical Society. It had taken him about two months of work over one year's time to complete up to his present point. Painting in acrylics, the mural seemed to be about sixty percent complete. Bill was a very friendly and talented fellow that had also crossed paths with Dayton Duncan when Dayton was filming at Fort Mandan during the winter of 1994. Well, to make a long story short, we had a longer and much more interesting stop than we had anticipated, but we finally got to the fort, which is just west of Washburn.

We did a good deal of exploring at Fort Mandan, a replica of the structure where the Lewis and Clark expedition spent the winter of 1804–1805 and met fifteen-year-old Sacagawea in the Mandan village across the river. She was a member of the Shoshoni nation by birth, was six months pregnant when they met, and ended up becoming an invaluable interpreter and guide for the party. Although her name has several spelling variations, Sacagawea, pronounced with a hard "g" sound, is now the most widely accepted. Fort Mandan has interior dimensions of seventeen paces wide and about twenty-six paces deep. It has a triangular floor plan, and the dimensions do not include the rooms on either side, which are about eight-and-a-half paces square. Imagine living in there all winter!

After walking around this replica of the fort, we got on the bikes at about 12:30 P.M. The Bianchi Project-5 was our choice for our bicycles. They are performance hybrids that incorporate a mountain bike frame geometry on a larger scale that will allow us to use both road and off-road tires on the same rims. Our goal was to take advantage of the bike's larger wheel size, which would be more efficient on the smooth pavement, and the durable frame and knobby tire option for our off-road rides. As we will be riding on many different surfaces, this choice will eliminate the need to transport, service and maintain both road and mountain bikes on the trip.

Todd and I were excited to be on the road at last, and we got off to a fine start on a sunny day. Packed in our panniers was a variety of items from sunscreen and water to tools, spare tubes and a cellular telephone. There was great scenery – rolling, undulating ground – and not the flat, monotonous land I had expected. One horse in a roadside pasture answered my imitated horse whinny, and this seemed like a good omen. The sun was hot, especially when we stopped riding. After passing through the little town of Stanton, we made a stop at Knife River Park. The remains of Indian lodges have been found here, so we checked them out and then continued on our way. Near the end of today's ride, we stopped

Fort Mandan

in the Lake Store/Grocery in Pick City, North Dakota . . . just about a mile and a half west of the Garrison Dam. Great water! Whew! Just what we needed! We knew we couldn't rest for long, so after a fifteen minute break, we were back on the road. We passed over the magnificent two-and-a-half-mile long Garrison Dam. Communication with the Rig was spotty, but we were able to arrange a pick up at the intersection of Route 200 and Highway 48.

We had a ten-minute ride in the Rig to Fort Stevenson State Park which is a beautiful site on Lake (reservoir) Sakakawea, another spelling version of Sacagawea. It was a tough ride today in the hottest part of the day, but we're interested to compare this with tomorrow.

MERIWETHER LEWIS – FORT MANDAN APRIL 7TH. 1805

Having on this day at 4. P.M. completed every arrangement necessary for our departure, . . . Capt. Clark emba[r]ked with our party and proceeded up the River. as I had used no exercise for several weeks, I determined to walk on shore as far as our encampment of this evening.

Our vessels consisted of six small canoes, and two large perogues. This little fleet altho' not quite so rispectable as those of Columbus or Capt. Cook, were still viewed by us with as much pleasure as those deservedly famed adventurers ever beheld theirs; and I dare say with quite as much anxiety for their safety and preservation. we were now about to penetrate a country at least two thousand miles in width, on which the foot of civilized man had never trodden; the good or evil it had in store for us was for experiment yet to determine. . . .

JUNE 24, 1994 – FRIDAY

OK, So we decided that today is the 24th. Days, dates and time don't seem to mean much out here. We drove to the intersection of Routes 37 and 1804, about twelve miles west of Garrison, ND. We started riding at 8:30 A.M. A good deal of this territory looks the same to the non-native eye, one long, undulating road after another stretching to the horizon. A fantastic, early morning ride was had past many cows and horses on endless rolling land. We stopped at a sharp, northerly turn in the road on Route 1804. The silence was absolutely stunning. It was amazing just to hear the uninterrupted sounds of nature, as there were no man-made sounds at all – no planes, tractors, cars, people, power lines and transformers – only the sounds of wind, insects, birds, cows and horses.

Two Power Bars were consumed today and lots of liquid. Stomach cramps started to bother me at about 10:30 A.M. There was an interesting Indian Scout Cemetery that we passed after entering the Fort Berthold Indian Reservation. While on the road, Todd and I passed the time by playing a game to see which one of us could most accurately guess the number of miles to the next horizon point. Nine to twelve miles seemed to be the average.

Gordon T. Ward

Lunch was at the Redwood Cafe in Parshall. Little did we know that Bob was eating lunch there as well. He was doing laundry down the street, too. I ordered two huge pancakes and hash browns. Todd got a cheeseburger platter with potato salad and an enormous vanilla shake – thirty-two ounces at least. The ride out of Parshall to New Town was very difficult for me. Hot weather, traffic and trucks on Route 23 made the going stressful, and my stomach cramps were getting worse.

New Town was a stop for us because of an interview we had with Jim Vranna at the *New Town News*. This was the largest town we've ridden through so far, yet it was still small by New Jersey standards. New Town was created when the towns of Elbow Woods, Sanish and Van Hook were flooded due to the rising waters of the Garrison Reservoir. After the interview, we rode out of town and were picked up two miles outside of New Town on Route 1804.

I had no dinner tonight except a small bowl of leftover spaghetti – my stomachache was bad. I took some tablets and will hope for the best tomorrow. I spent the night writing post cards. A brief rain shower occurred at 10:00 P.M., reemphasizing the wide, wild, free and unpopulated area around us.

This expansive and seemingly endless land is forcing me to notice that the monotony one can feel in any given environment can be overcome by appreciating simplicity, looking a little deeper and taking notice of the minutia. I try to make a mental list the things I have done throughout the day. In this way I can gauge how attentive I am to the world around me. Remember how time seemed to go slower when you were young? I believe this is due to the fact that everything was new and everything was an adventure. As adults, we need to reawaken our sense of wonder. Cultivating and developing an acute awareness and appreciation of our surroundings is the key to a more fulfilled life. We have become so focused on the glitz, the action, and the monumental accomplishments in this modern world that we have neglected the simple gifts which surround us on a continual basis. Every breath is a gift. Every time we open our eyes we are given a unique perspective on the world, which goes largely unnoticed or unappreciated. Notice the small, minute details and you will see a world anew in a microcosm. Feel the gentle breeze amidst the whirlwind of appointments. Look for pennies in a land of wealth. Appreciate the common place events. Contemplate the light from one star in the neon world. Know that your thoughts and your senses are the focal points in the confusion of society and the often hurried pace of modern life.

North Dakota road

morning preparation

WILLIAM CLARK – JULY 26TH FRIDAY 1805
. . . I felt my Self verry unwell & took up Camp on the little river . . .

JUNE 25, 1994 – SATURDAY

We headed out of Lewis and Clark State Park. It was a clean and well run place to camp. My stomach cramps were still there but not as bad as yesterday, so I decided to see how far I could make it. It was sunny but very windy from a strong headwind that we would be riding into today. The Rig took us to Route 1804, and we biked about eighteen miles to Williston, ND where we satisfied our craving for carbohydrates with doughnuts at a local bakery called Sticky Fingers. Excellent! From there we followed Rt. 1804 through Trenton to Fort Buford Historical Site. Sitting Bull and Chief Joseph were two notable people that were imprisoned here.

Next to this site was the confluence of the Missouri and Yellowstone Rivers. This was a significant Lewis and Clark point, because it is where the two explorers reconvened after splitting up on their return journey. Lewis had gone north of the Missouri into Blackfeet territory, and Clark traveled south along the Yellowstone. Bob had some fun here by following a ground squirrel with his camera. Mr. Squirrel proved to be most photogenic. Two miles down the road was the North Dakota/Montana state line, and we stopped to have our picture taken by the sign.

Following a dirt road up to Bainville and past Fort Union was one of the most exciting riding experiences to date. It followed train tracks where we were passed by five freight trains during this part of the ride. The traffic control for trains out here must be like air traffic control. Hmm, perhaps a little less stressful. Todd saw a rock formation that looked like a pharaoh on one of the cliffs lining the right side of the road. I thought it looked like an Indian head. At any event, we both photographed it, so that we could point out the different features to each other at a later date.

At the end of the dirt/gravel road, we climbed into the Rig and rode to Fort Peck, so we would have time to ride around Fort Peck Lake and check out the campground. It wasn't

confluence of the Yellowstone and Missouri Rivers

long before we were cruisin' through Wolf Point with Emmy Lou Harris on the radio. What more could you ask for? We did have our first buffalo sighting while we were in the RV this afternoon. One, solitary buffalo was grazing not far from the side of the road just inside the Montana border on Route 2 west of Bainville. We also saw a tumbleweed on our ride this morning while we were on route 1804 coming into Williston, North Dakota. It's pretty flat out here. So . . . Todd, Bob, me and Emmy Lou were headin' for Fort Peck.

We pulled into a campground just below the Fort Peck Dam. The evening was spent eating, changing our sets of road tires to knobby tires and looking at the proposed route and time schedule for the Fort Peck Lake section of the trip.

North Dakota/Montana state line

WILLIAM CLARK – MAY 22ND WEDNESDAY 1805

The wind continued to blow so violently hard we did not think it prudent to set out untill it luled a little. . . .

MERIWETHER LEWIS – MONDAY SEPTEMBER 17TH. 1804.

This senery already rich pleasing and beatiful was still farther hightened by immense herds of Buffaloe, deer Elk and Antelopes which we saw in every direction feeding on the hills and plains. I do not think I exagerate when I estimate the number of Buffaloe which could be compre[hend]ed at one view to amount to 3000.

JUNE 26, 1994 – SUNDAY

What a magnificent Sunday! We packed at Fort Peck and, after much disagreement and uncertainty about when to ride because of reports of thunderstorms and dangerous hail, we left at 2:30 P.M. We had waited because the last storm of the magnitude that was currently forecasted was accompanied by grapefruit-sized hail that damaged roofs and cars, not to mention what it could do to people.

Our ride began at the intersection of Seventh Ridge Road and Willow Creek Road with an expansive, 360° horizon and no trace of any other people. It was sunny when we began, but a ridge of clouds in the west signaled the approaching storm front. One half hour into our ride, it hit. Dust storms blew hard up the once seemingly endless dirt road, shortening their linear character with grey and brown haze. Todd and I pulled into a grass covered "road," indicated only by tire marks which flattened the existing grass. Wind hammered away at the formless tent, turning it into a sail which we desperately fought to erect. Grey-black clouds suffocated the once blue skies above us and to the west. One is quickly reminded how small we are compared to the awesome power of nature on this open grazing rangeland. Finally the tent was up, and we hurriedly threw our panniers inside to weigh it down. Sandblasted bikes were dragged behind the tent to shield them from the wind-driven dirt, and we crawled inside the stretched fabric form that was being battered and pushed to one side by the storm – still no rain, just the constant driving wind.

As we looked out the tent door we noticed an incredible occurrence. The storm started to move in a clockwise pattern above our tent leaving clear skies above us. We were being miraculously spared and only received a few sprinkles as we watched violent lightning strikes and sheets of rain fall to the south, north and east upon the open rangeland. Although the wind never stopped, Pasta Roma was cooked for an evening meal, and we had an unbelievably entertaining/frightening/hysterical time chasing the free roaming, open range cattle away from our tent. They were extremely curious and much bigger than us!

Another spectacular gift was given to us in the form of an unexpected sunset which contrasted the brightly lit, golden buttes to the east against the dark, grey skies – stunning and breathtaking! This is a moment that you have to experience to truly appreciate, and we were fortunate to have been given a chance to view it. We thought we were going to get hammered by a storm, and we didn't. I feel as though an unseen presence is guarding us.

After a long and varied day, we went to bed at 9:45 P.M. because we plan to get up early and make it to Sun Prairie. I fear we haven't escaped the storm in its entirety, as the skies

windblown tent in storm north of Fort Peck Lake

campsite north of Fort Peck Lake

have begun to look more menacing again after sunset. It is hard to describe the total isolation and vulnerability that one feels out here.

MERIWETHER LEWIS – SUNDAY JULY 28TH 1805

. . . in the evening about 4 O'Ck the wind blew hard from the South West and after some little time brought on a Cloud attended with thunder and Lightning from which we had a fine refreshing shower which cooled the air considerably; the showers continued with short intervals untill after dark.

MERIWETHER LEWIS – WEDNESDAY MAY 29TH 1805

Last night we were all allarmed by a large buffaloe Bull, which swam over from the opposite shore and coming along side of the white perogue, climbed over it to land,   he then allarmed ran up the bank in full speed directly towards the fires, and was within 18 inches of the heads of some of the men who lay sleeping. . . .

MERIWETHER LEWIS – SUNDAY JUNE 2ND 1805.

The wind blew violently last night and was attended by a slight shower of rain. . . .

JUNE 27, 1994 – MONDAY

Melina turned seven years old today, and I wished terribly that I could have been there. Happy birthday, Mina! I did not sleep well during the night and thought constantly about the possibility of getting to a phone, so I could call her on her birthday.

The rain showers were intermittent during the night, but the rain which had died off in the early evening of the 26th, resumed their fury around 2:30 A.M. The rain on the tent was a very lonely sound, and we both felt extremely isolated. A vehicle of some sort drove past us at 4:30 A.M. We were in our tent and did not see it, but we wondered where the person might be headed in such a lonesome and far removed area.

I got up at 4:59 A.M., as did Todd, and we cooked a breakfast of oatmeal. The sky was grey, and the wind was driving and consistent. After we ate, we donned our rain gear, packed, and started dismantling our tent. Suddenly the sound of an engine was heard, and a yellow pickup truck came over the rise and pulled into our site. A weathered-looking man that exuded a confidence of the surrounding area rolled down his window and asked, "What are you doing way the hell out here?" I explained that we were caught in the storm, and we described the ordeal we had setting up the site. We asked about the road leading to Sun Prairie, and the man's response was, "Nooo, I don't think they use that road anymore." Needless to say this piece of information was to make all the difference in our trip, since we would have surely run into problems with our intended route. We were given directions for a more traveled route, whatever "traveled" meant. Anyway, we noted his directions, and, before he drove off, we asked him where he was going. "To work!" was his reply, and he drove off into the early morning light. Where he could possibly work in the middle of open rangeland was a mystery to us, but we were to be given an answer very soon. Our chance meeting would come to be viewed by myself as one which seemed to have been arranged by fate. If I was not convinced about the existence of angels at this point, I would soon be faced with a series of events that would make me reconsider.

Todd and I finished dismantling our weather-beaten tent, packed our belongings and headed west on the muddy Willow Creek Road. Our first mile was rough because of the relentless headwind in our face. When we came to the intersection with the road to Sun Prairie, and I use the term "intersection" very loosely, we spotted the yellow truck that our early morning visitor had been driving, but there was no sign of him anywhere. At any rate, we took the advice that he had given us earlier and turned right, heading up the alternate, serpentine, dirt road named Stone House Road. Todd and I were prepared for the fact that we would not see any paved roads for a couple of days, but this dirt was thick from the rain, and it stuck to our tires like glue. The local folks call this mud "gumbo."

About three hundred yards up this road, we encountered our first piece of "bad luck" for the day. My rear tire had gone flat, and we were forced to stop while I unpacked my gear and removed the rear wheel and tire. Of course, the wind was still blowing hard, the skies were still overcast, and we were hoping that it would not rain during this episode. The dirt, which I had mentioned earlier, now stuck to everything it touched, and the most maddening part was trying to keep our cleats from becoming encased in it. Of course, our efforts were in vain. I tried three times to patch the inner tube but had no luck in getting the patch to stick. It was also very difficult to determine where the leaks were, as the sound of escaping air from the inner tube was easily drowned out by the wind.

During the last try, Todd spotted a vehicle in the distance that seemed to be coming our way, albeit very slowly. We continued working but kept an eye on whatever was approaching because it didn't seem to be a car. Finally it got close enough for us to deter-

changing a tire on Stone House Road

mine that it was a road grader. Apparently, someone had the job of scraping all of the foot high weeds off of the crest of the road. When it got to us, it stopped, and we saw that the driver was none other than our morning visitor. He shook his head, took the cigarette from his mouth and asked us if we needed help. With blind pride, Todd and I both thanked him but said that we would be fine. Actually, we had already decided to scrap the original inner tube and replace it with a new one. Our friend nodded in acceptance and continued his seemingly endless grading. Our new tubes ended up being a little too small, but this one worked, at least for the time being. Todd and I sipped some water, which was getting low after a day of no water sources, reassembled my bike and resumed our riding, thinking how odd it was to have met the same man in less than a few hours in this unpopulated environment. Both times he showed up when he was or might have been needed most.

Our new route presented two problems. One was the additional miles, which we would have to peddle in order to make it to the James Kipp Recreation Area by tomorrow afternoon. That alone was a considerable obstacle considering the vicious headwinds that were seriously hampering our progress. The second issue was that neither Bob nor anyone else would know our new route should we run into trouble. We had been forced to cut our support line in order to make it to our next designated meeting point. This all meant that we had to push ourselves hard to make up the miles, and we had to be very careful in the process.

All day we rode into the same headwind, and, although the skies cleared, we were growing more and more concerned about our situation. We were surrounded in every direction and as far as we could see by rolling terrain that was covered by grey rock, brown dirt and yellow clover. Nowhere was there any sign of water. The wind often changed direction but not intensity, so our tire tracks looked like the tracks of snakes, crisscrossing the road as if we were drunken men.

Just as we gained stability with one direction of the wind, it would shift and slam into us from another direction. The combination of the hills, an increasing lack of water, an even more increasing desire to drink, and the variable wind sapped our strength quickly. Our two-way radio would not reach Bob, and there were no cells in the area to carry the signal for the cellular phone. Except for our friend working in the road grader, we had not seen another person, or the sign of another person, all day. As we were told, "No one goes out there." All we could do was plod onward and look forward to the chance that the place marked Stone House on our map would have a phone. Six hours after we had started our ride, we had

Stone House Road – windy and dry!

covered only 10.67 miles, averaging 1.94 miles per hour in vicious headwinds. At one point Todd got off of his bike as we were climbing a hill and kept pace with me by walking as I rode. There was nothing that could have prepared us for this, and the emotional drain was tremendous because of the uncertainty of our route and the urgency of our situation.

As we came over the top of one of the many hills, we saw what we had been hoping to see . . . water! It wasn't much. In fact, it was only a drainage pool about thirty yards in diameter, but it was water. We worked our way down the hill into the wind and wasted no time getting the water purifier pump out of the pannier. As we worked our way through the ankle deep mud that surrounded the drainage pool, we noticed a pair of American Avocet birds, which we had disturbed. They flew around the pool of water constantly, nervously landing for only a few seconds before taking to flight again. They were interesting birds to see as they resembled large sandpipers with long, curved beaks and blue legs. They most likely had a nest in the area. Anyway, Todd volunteered to walk into the water far enough to get to a depth where the purifier would work. This was a new purifier which had been used only once by Todd after he ordered it. Imagine our total disbelief when it would not work correctly. Water spurted out of the top of the unit instead of running through the tube.

Emotions ran the gamut from frustration to infuriation and from contemplation to fright as we considered our situation – windy, 90° heat, no form of communication for help, and no water. To drink the unpurified water would mean running the risk of contracting Giardia, an intestinal virus, which would certainly end the journey for both of us. To not drink any water would mean serious trouble, and we tried not to think about it. We certainly didn't talk about it, but we could see the worry in each other's eyes.

Getting back to my earlier comment on angels. A series of events, which had played themselves out unbeknownst to us, was about to affect us in a wondrous manner. As Todd and I were feeling about as frightened and discouraged as we had ever been, I looked up the road to see a spectacular sight. Coming over the rise was an RV, our Rig, which paused at the top of the hill so that Bob could get out and take a photograph of us.

Even he did not yet know the gravity of our situation and how well timed his unexpected appearance was.

As soon as we got our thirst quenched, we asked Bob how he found us. Apparently the storm from the previous night had missed us but had hammered other locations with torrential rains, violent lightning and heavy winds. Bob became extremely worried for our safety

our drainage pool / water source

and set out looking for us this morning. He followed our designated route, only to find, as we had been told, that the road was closed. Retracing his route, Bob remarkably happened to pass our morning visitor who was still at work grading the dirt roads. Not only did Bob stop to speak with him, but because of our meeting earlier in the morning, our friend recognized us by Bob's descriptions, told him where we were headed, described our route and said that we had had problems with our tires. Had it not been for that gentleman in the pickup truck on his way to work, we would have been in a very grave situation. He was the only person that would have known our whereabouts. Were all of these events coincidences? We felt very fortunate, and I again sensed the comforting impression that someone was watching over us.

We headed toward Saco in the Rig. It was amazing to see how differently Todd and I now viewed the environment. It suddenly took on a beautiful, scenic quality that had not impressed us before. Along the way, we saw a rattlesnake on the dusty road, a reminder of the other risks involved with our trip. We did pass that place called Stone House. It is a good thing that we didn't depend upon this location for a telephone and water, for it was not a town. It was, as the name suggested, a stone house. We saw some horses but no people.

Finally we got to Saco and had to fill up on gas, which was becoming another concern of ours for a time. We saw no place for lunch, so we continued driving to a town called Malta. Our rule for eating was one that we adopted from our friend Dayton Duncan, who had driven the Lewis and Clark Trail. The best places to eat are those that have someone's name on the sign. No chain or franchise restaurants are allowed, but diners are acceptable. There was a diner in Malta that had a casino attached to it. Understand that this was not your Las Vegas/Atlantic City type of casino. These establishments reminded me more of bowling alleys, and slot machines were the main attraction. Todd and I had burgers, fries and shakes, and what a welcome sight they were! After eating, I called The Sports People in Bedminster, New Jersey and asked them to send tubes that might better fit our off-road tires. They agreed to send them to the outfitter where we would soon arrive for our Missouri River canoe trip.

Again, it was time to drive, and we headed down to the James Kipp Recreation Area. It took a while, but we arrived in the mid-afternoon. This gave us time to look around the scenic campsite and take in some time beside the river. Magpies were very abundant here and were stunning with their black and white coloring.

Todd and I plan to bike east along the river tomorrow in order to take in some of the sights that we would have seen on our original route. This meant cleaning our bikes before dinner, since they were covered with red dust from our ride out of the Fort Peck rangeland. After dealing with a drainage problem in the RV's shower and organizing our gear for tomorrow's overnight trip, I am certain that we are all looking forward to a solid night's sleep!

MERIWETHER LEWIS – FRIDAY JUNE 7TH 1805. -

It continued to rain almost without intermission last night and as I expected we had a most disagreeable and wrestless night. Our camp possessing no allurements, we left our watery beads at an early hour and continued our rout . . . it still continues to rain the wind hard from the N.E. . . . the ground remarkably, slipry . . . notwithstanding the rain that has now fallen the earth of these bluffs is not wet to a greater debth than 2 inches; in it's present state it is precisely like walking over frozen growned which is thawed to small debth and slips equally as bad. this clay not only appears to require more water to saturate it as I before observed than any earth I ever observed but when saturated it appears on the other hand to yield it's moisture with equal difficulty.

WILLIAM CLARK – MAY 30TH THURSDAY 1805

The rain commenced yesterday evining, and continued moderately through the course of the night, more rain has now fallin than we have experienced since the 15th of September last, the rain continued this morning, and the wind too high for us to proceed, untill about 11 oClock at which time we set out, and proceeded on with great labour. . . .

MERIWETHER LEWIS – FRIDAY JULY 26TH 1805.

. . . the high lands are thin meager soil covered with dry low sedge and a species of grass also dry the seeds of which are armed with a long twisted hard beard at the upper extremity . . .

WILLIAM CLARK – MAY 22ND WEDNESDAY 1805

. . . a verry rich stickey soil producing but little vegetation of any kind except the prickley pear, but little grass & that verry low.

Our first order of business today was calling a Portland radio station that had wanted to track our progress once we got a significant distance into Montana. This was an enjoyable phone call. One of the things we found out right away was the correct pronunciation of Oregon. We gave away our eastern upbringing by having to be told that the state was pronounced OR-E-G'N, not OR-E-GONE!

After the call, we began our riding. We rode out of James Kipp Recreation Area and went thirty-five miles east into the Charles M. Russell National Wildlife Refuge and along the Missouri River on a sand/dirt road that meandered, climbed and descended along the riverside. It was a beautiful day . . . no wind, bright sunshine, no clouds in the sky. We expected an excellent day, but it quickly became apparent how hot it was going to be, even along the water. Some of the ruts in the sandy sections of the road made for tricky riding, and I went down once while descending a heavily gullied section, bruising only my pride. For a break, we ate lunch and rested under some pines. We had decided to try the water pump again because we had it working at our campsite last night. However, Murphy's Law was not to be suppressed because we found to our disappointment that it did not work once we were on our own again. There was a roadside pool where we got to drink partially purified and filtered water. I don't know if we got good water or not, but we'll find out on July 4th, a week from today. Subsequent entries may come from a men's room someplace. Later on, we also boiled river water but didn't need to drink it. Relief from the heat was wading into four-inch deep water. The river was amazingly shallow at the point where we stopped riding. A dozen or so pelicans took off from the river, and I spotted two more that were floating down current. It was strange how perfect they appeared, almost as if they were artificial.

Doubling back and weary from the heat and a hard ride up and over a steep grade on sand roads, we finally found a place to camp that is two hours east of tomorrow's pick-up point. Our campsite is on a bluff overlooking the river and is quite scenic.

There are beavers in the water and millions of mosquitoes to annoy us. I am forced to wear my rain gear to keep them off of me. Thankfully, the river was deeper here, and both of us had a chance to swim after sliding and scrambling down the sandy cliffs in front of our campsite. The water felt wonderful! Todd and I remain very thirsty, even after swimming. As I sit inside the tent watching a gorgeous moonrise over the water, I am torn between the

river bluff campsite in the Charles M. Russell National Wildlife Refuge

apparent foolishness of trusting the integrity of our water filter and the fact that this sight was worth the risk. After all, we will only need to ride for two hours early tomorrow morning. Earlier tonight, packs of coyotes could be heard in two different directions. One pack was on the opposite bank of the river. The other was on our side and appeared to be coming toward our tent, but they never arrived. We were visited only by their high, mournful cries. It was exciting all the same, and it reminded me of Lewis and Clark, as they were the first from our country to see a coyote.

MERIWETHER LEWIS – FRIDAY JULY 12TH 1805.

Musquetoes extreemly troublesome to me today nor is a large knat less troublesome which does not sting, but attacks the eye in swarms and compells us to brush them off or have our eyes filled with them.

WEDNESDAY, JUNE 29, 1994

This was Hell Day. We're still thirsty, and I would have given just about anything for a diet Coke. Todd and I got going early . . . 4:30 wake-up and on the road by 6:00 A.M. to avoid sweating with the sun and losing water from our bodies. Our riding frightened a herd of cattle from the thick, yellow clover that grows on both sides of the road we were on. All of them raced for the road and ran in front of us, as we unwittingly conducted our first cattle drive. Unfortunately, the clover, as beautiful as it is, holds concerns for the local ranchers. Not only is it a fire hazard when it grows in such copious amounts, it also will give the cattle colic if they eat too much of it. To our dismay we experienced the effects of this problem first hand. These cows had diarrhea, and, since we could not ride off the road due to the thick, chest high undergrowth, we were forced to ride through the tracks, piles and puddles left behind by the cattle. Not only did it smell bad, but the sensation of the drying cow excrement that clung to us is not something I would like to repeat. Eventually the cattle turned off the road, and we plodded ahead. Finally we got to the boat ramp, our pick-up point, at 9:00 A.M. and waited until 2:30, the scheduled time for Bob to pick us up. We swam when we could, but I mostly

relief from the heat

sat under a dilapidated picnic table, avoiding the sun and dreaming of a cold drink.

I was very hot and cranky. The horseflies were relentless. The water was nice, but I didn't have the energy to get up and go in there. At least the vultures weren't circling! Both of us were dehydrated at this point. It was like being in a daze. I even had periods of time when I imagined Todd talking to me, and I would ask him, in confusion, what it was that he had said. Later, I calculated that I drank eighty-four ounces or so of liquid in between our pick-up time and bed at 11:00 P.M.

After Bob picked us up, we drove to Judith Landing, passing an old schoolhouse where we stopped to take some photographs.

Toward late afternoon we arrived at our destination, the PN Ranch, where we were invited to spend the night by the owner, Dan Todd. We were introduced to Dan's nephew Jeb and Dan's friend Barbara. Dan drove us around in his Jeep for a tour of his ranch, and we learned that Lewis and Clark camped on the banks of the Missouri that are now part of Dan's property. Later, Todd went along for a ride in Dan's single-engine airplane in order to pick up a lemon meringue pie from a neighboring ranch. It seems that most ranchers need to have the use of a plane in order to keep track of their cattle. The planes are also handy in spotting

old Montana schoolhouse

brush fires, which are fought by all available hands in the area. Fire control is a genuine, joint effort, and Jeb was just cleaning up from a recent fire fight when we arrived at the ranch.

In the evening, we were all treated to an excellent meal of meat and potatoes. I especially enjoyed the "Todd Family Salad." The dressing ingredients were: balsamic vinegar, oil, garlic, apricot jam, choke cherry jam and raspberry jam, some lemon juice and some salt and pepper. The salad itself consisted of: mushrooms, apples, sunflower seeds, some scallions and an assortment of lettuces. It was excellent! We have to make it at home.

After finishing up our laundry, we turned in for a good night's sleep. Barbara will be driving us to the boat launch tomorrow at 7:00 A.M. We should be there by 9:00 A.M.

I have to mention an interesting gravesite that we were shown on Dan's property. The grave belongs to a man, referred to as Uncle Mat, who came out west from New York City to kill an Indian before they were all gone. His real name was Mat Duncan. Mat was himself killed by Indians before he could kill any of them. His simple tombstone reads:

MAT DUNCAN | KILLED | BY Indians | APRIL 2d | 1881 | aged 21Yrs | Residence | N.Y.C.

Bad karma got him! Justice at its best.

SERGEANT PATRICK GASS – MONDAY [MAY] 27TH [1805]
. . . the most dismal country I ever beheld. . . .

Thursday, June 30, 1994

We began our river trip today. Breakfast was at the PN Ranch. Eggs, potatoes, toast and waffles was the fare. Barbara drove us to Virgelle after leaving the Rig at the Judith Landing/PN Bridge next to Dan's property. We got our canoes and supplies at the Virgelle Mercantile and set out from Coal Banks Landing on part of the Wild and Scenic section of the Missouri River. A Killdeer was spotted on the side of the river two miles south of Coal Banks landing, and we also saw a young golden eagle, which was pretty spectacular.

Beautiful day – current of two to three mph. All three of us were immediately struck by the calm and stillness of this river environment.

We paddled up to an island in the middle of the river for lunch and later made a stop at White Rocks, a rock formation that was noted by Lewis and Clark.

We beached our canoes and explored on foot in this fantastic area. This site offers spectacular sights and rock formations. It was like being in a Star Trek scene. These white, rock walls incorporate grotesquely shaped areas which resemble faces, statues and gargoyles. Other sections look like the ruins of ancient fortresses and cities, but they were all naturally formed.

paddling on the Missouri River

beginning of the White Rocks section of the Missouri River

With all this molded rock and towering white sandstone all around you . . . set off by the blue sky . . . it's impossible not to be filled with a sense of awe. Many photos were taken here.

We continued paddling fifteen miles down to a spot where we would spend the night. It was also a Lewis and Clark campsite on May 31, 1805, and it was here that we had our first dinner: cheese and crackers, pork chops, rice, applesauce, Snickers and soda. Wow! Today's lunch was equally as good with taco salad, juice boxes and cookies. We met a group at the campsite this evening that was led by a roommate of Dan Todd's. He is leading a group of Lewis and Clark experts from the Snake River Institute. This is a great and much anticipated section of our trip, as we are seeing and traveling the way Lewis and Clark did. Tomorrow promises to offer even more historical and significant sites.

I am looking at a monumental rock formation from our campsite across the river. It is a mammoth, black, towering structure called LaBarge Rock, and it is named after Joseph LaBarge, a steamboat pilot. One lone tree grows atop, and fir trees line the crevasse on the right side which rises directly out of the Missouri. It is symbolic to me as representing the determination, isolation and significance of the original journey.

natural rock walls along the Missouri River

Today was the first day I wore Melina's hat, and I left it at White Rocks. Todd and I paddled upstream for a half mile to recover it, as I had promised Melina that I would take care of it. Actually, the hat has been a great emotional connection to home for me. Apparently, I also left my watch in Barbara's car. Maybe I will get it back on Saturday if she finds it. I miss Melina a great deal and am counting the days 'till I see her. This is much harder being separated than I would have imagined. I am losing a month out of my child's life. Is it worth the trade for this experience? The answer I would give depends upon my current mood. Even though I am having a wonderful time and accomplishing a great deal for a worthy cause, I would give anything to hug Melina and share my experiences with her. I suppose that if this realization were to be the only thing gained from the trip, then it has to be considered a success, for I will hold Melina nearer and dearer to my heart when I return. Like the lone tree on the cliff summit, this trip is a precarious emotional situation. An ecology of the heart will be the best response. I can't wait to call home on Saturday!

Note: John Shields, a blacksmith and a gunsmith and a member of the Lewis and Clark expedition's permanent party, was a thirty-five-year-old married man. He and his wife Nancy had a daughter named Janette. Being exactly thirty-five years old myself, I wonder what his feelings were about being away from home.

P.S. No Giardia symptoms yet!

MERIWETHER LEWIS – FRIDAY MAY 31, 1805. -

The hills and river Clifts which we passed today exhibit a most romantic appearance. The bluffs of the river rise to the hight of from 2 to 300 feet and in most places nearly perpendicular; they are formed of remarkable white sandstone which is sufficiently soft to give way readily to the impression of water; . . . The water in the course of time in decending from those hills and plains on either side of the river has trickled down the soft sand clifts and woarn it into a thousand grotesque figures, which with the help of a little imagination and an oblique view, at a distance are made to represent eligant ranges of lofty freestone buildings, having their parapets well stocked with statuary; collumns of various sculpture both grooved and plain, are also seen supporting long galleries in front of those buildings; . . . on these clifts I met with a species of pine which I had never seen, it differs from the pitch-pine in the particular of it's leaf and cone, the first being vastly shorter, and the latter considerably longer and more pointed.

FRIDAY, JULY 1, 1994:

The following entries for this date were transcribed from an audio journal. No written journal entries were made on this day due to an illness that will be explained later.

ENTRY #1: JULY 1ST, FRIDAY MORNING. Woke up at camp at about 6:00 A.M. It's a beautiful day, and it's going to be hot again. We had a breakfast with some pancakes, sausage, eggs and orange juice. It's now eight o'clock, and we're all packed up and ready to go. We'll be headin' down river to another campsite which is about twenty-one miles from here. So, we just have to stuff our gear in the canoes, and we'll be off.

ENTRY #2: We're headin' down the river by Pablo Island. The rock formations are incredible with names such as Citadel Rock and Steamboat Rock. Apparently these unique landforms were used as natural landmarks for steamboat pilots during the late 19th and early 20th centuries.

It's become an incredible struggle for me just to stay awake. We have about five more miles to go before our campsite, moving at about two and a half to three miles per hour. We should be there in, I guess, a couple hours or so. Just saw two mule deer on the side of the river. See ya!

rock formation along the Missouri River

Part 3

Western Montana

I have been sick for the past four days, so I haven't been writing entries since June 30, 1994. I became ill on July 1st after pulling into our second campsite on the river. My symptoms range from extreme dizziness to thirst, fever, lack of energy and muscle cramps. Occasional nausea also occurs. I spent all of Friday afternoon and evening lying on the ground with my head propped up on a river bag. That night it again became very apparent how vulnerable we were. My thoughts were on my family, and I would have given anything to have been home at that point. The thought of getting up and traveling the remaining twelve miles to the PN Bridge by canoe seemed impossible for me to handle. However, when Saturday morning came, a spot was made for me to lie in the canoe, and Todd paddled me into the bridge.

I felt like a burden, but I deeply appreciate all that Todd and Bob did to help me. After we arrived, we picked up our bikes at the PN Ranch and headed to Fort Benton in the Rig. I visited the medical center there and was told that I was probably dehydrated and had the flu. We also got a prescription to treat Giardia in case we got it later in the trip. Judy, the

off to the hospital

RN, and Dr. Michael Whiting were very helpful. We checked into the Fort Benton Motel for the night, and it felt good to be in a bed with sheets instead of a sleeping bag. It was also the opportunity to make the most needed phone call that I made home. Melina will never realize how comforting her voice was to hear. It made me miss her more than I had previously.

Looking back over the past few days, much has happened. The river trip, while it had its moments of awesome spectacle, was sluggish, still and hot with a silence at times that was broken only by the sound of our paddles stroking the water. The river speed was two-and-a-half mph, sometimes with a headwind, and cows lined many of the banks. The food provided to us was copious in quantity – too much in fact. One of the more stimulating parts of the trip occurred early on Thursday. We spent about forty-five minutes at a spot called the White Rocks which I described in my Thursday, June 30, 1994 journal entry.

Yesterday, Sunday, found me feeling not too much improved. Bob and Todd had breakfast, and we all drove to Great Falls with me feeling very uncomfortable in the upper bunk section of the RV. We checked into Dick's RV Park where we spent the night. We did visit the Fort Benton emergency room one more time before our drive to Great Falls to discuss places to buy Pedialite. I needed to get my electrolytes in synch and all the pharmacies were closed. We ended up buying it in the Fort Benton IGA.

On Monday I awoke feeling much better. I had found that eating actually made my stomach feel better on Sunday night when I forced myself to have Oodles of Noodles, soup and toast. So, when Monday rolled around, we all went across the street from the RV park to a restaurant called Elmer's that specializes in pancakes. I had a short stack of four blueberry pancakes (seven inches in diameter). A full stack was six! It stayed down, and I continued to improve throughout the day although my temperature fluctuated between 99° and 101.9°. By the end of the day I felt well enough to do some much needed bike maintenance. Road tires had to be put on our wheels, and the caked dust needed to be cleaned out of the crevasses of the bikes. Dinner consisted of chicken, assorted frozen veggies and rice. Since this was the Fourth of July, fireworks and firecrackers could be heard all around the RV park that night. Fireworks are apparently legal in Montana.

I feel like I am extra baggage for Bob and Todd because there is not much that I have the energy to do, and my symptoms seem to run in cycles with no predictability. It's all very frustrating!

MERIWETHER LEWIS – SATURDAY JULY 27TH 1805. -

Capt Clark arrived very sick with a high fever on him and much fatiegued and exhausted. he informed me that he was very sick all last night had a high fever and frequent chills & constant aking pains in all his mustles. . . . I prevailed on him to bath his feet in warm water and rest himself.

MERIWETHER LEWIS – SUNDAY JULY 28TH 1805.

I had our baggage spread out to dry this morning; and the day proving warm, I had a small bower or booth erected for the comfort of Capt. C.

TUESDAY, JULY 5, 1994, GREAT FALLS, MONTANA

I realized that I had to go to the emergency room today at Great Falls if I still felt badly. Surprisingly, I woke up feeling great, bounded out of bed and headed for the showers. This was a welcome change because I have been so depressed for the past several days. When I got into the shower, I checked the "bruise" on my right hip that I thought I must have gotten when I fell off the bike on the James Kipp trail ride a week before. I was amazed to see that it had increased in circular size to a diameter of about ten inches. What's more, it had a darker ring with about a two-inch diameter inside of it. Suddenly it all fit into place. The quirky flu symptoms I had been suffering could be those of Lyme Disease.

We promptly went to the Great Falls hospital, and I checked into the E.R. to have a doctor look at the rash and give me his opinion. The doctor informed me that there have not been any confirmed cases of Lyme Disease in Montana. As the disease needs ten days to produce a rash, there is a strong possibility that I was bitten at home. In any event, having come from the northeast where Lyme Disease is common, this was a situation where I had a different expectation concerning a quick diagnosis of the symptoms than those around me in the hospital. The doctor informed me that the treatment book indicated an EKG had to be administered before anything could be prescribed. The EKG came out fine, and I was prescribed Doxycycline. The doctor and I began talking about Quest West, and it turned out that he and his son had just completed the same Missouri River trip a number of weeks ago. He loved it! In fact, his son said that it was "just like Disneyland but without the crowds." It's strange how different people can have totally different reactions to the same events. Anyway, I left feeling much better knowing that I could put a name to my sickness.

After visiting the E.R., we drove around the area to see some sights before beginning our ride to Holter Lake. During our drive, we visited the Great Falls of the Missouri, which now has a dam at the site. Lewis and Clark were in the Great Falls area for thirty-two days, making this their longest stay in one place other than their winter camp sites. The explorers were expecting to have to navigate only one cascade, which would force a portage of no more than one half of a mile, a feat they planned to accomplished in a day. What they encountered were five waterfalls and a series of portages which took them two weeks to cover a distance they would normally travel by water in a single day. The falls, in the order they were reached going up river, were the Great Falls (highest of the series at eighty-nine feet), Horseshoe or Crooked Falls, Rainbow or Handsome Falls, Colter Falls (no longer visible and about a half mile up river from Rainbow Falls) and Black Eagle Falls (the second highest with a drop of some fifty feet).

Giant Springs was another stop for us. William Clark discovered this huge "fountain or spring" on June 18, 1805 during the portage around the Great Falls. Lewis later said it was the largest he had ever seen, and perhaps the largest in America. Giant Springs is appropriately named due to its rate of flow of nearly eight million gallons per hour. The water comes up from the Madison limestone formations which lie beneath most of central and eastern Montana. The springs today appear as a big concrete basin filled with water.

Our final sightseeing stop was to view a statue of Lewis, Clark, York and Seaman, Lewis's Newfoundland dog, which we used as a photo opportunity.

After this it was back to biking. Apparently the Doxycycline began working its magic very quickly. I felt much stronger, and I was eager to resume riding. Our bike ride to Holter Lake was spectacular – flat or downhill all the way. It meandered along railroad tracks and farmland and through magnificent canyons. The animal life that we saw included pelicans, eagles, mule deer, a black squirrel and hawks. Along the way, we struck up a conversation with a Montana Highway Patrol Officer (state police). His name was Fred Nowakowski, and we were surprised to learn that he was originally from Somerville, NJ! We talked at length about life in Montana vs. New Jersey. The pace of life is much more manageable out here in Montana. He told us some interesting stories about the tickets he's written for speeders from a notable auto magazine and others that use the area as a road testing site. Most of the people that received the tickets were amazed to discover, including Todd and me, that the fine for speeding, at any speed, is $5.00 and NO points. Unbelievable! Fred was the epitome of western hospitality. As we prepared to resume our ride, he gave us directions to his house and told us we were welcome to let ourselves in, rest, and get ourselves something to drink. We ended up declining his offer, needing to get some more miles under our belts, but we were very appreciative all the same.

Our day ended at the Holter Lake Campground where it poured rain all night and got rather chilly. Actually, the sound of rain makes for a peaceful sleeping sound. We have yet to ride through a hard rain and are considering ourselves very lucky.

Lewis and Clark statue in Great Falls, Montana

MERIWETHER LEWIS – FRIDAY JUNE 14TH 1805

    . . . hearing a tremendous roaring above me I continued my rout across the point of a hill a few hundred yards further and was again presented by one of the most beatifull objects in nature, a cascade of about fifty feet perpendicular stretching at rightangles across the river from side to side to the distance of at least a quarter of a mile. . . . I now thought that if a skillfull painter had been asked to make a beautifull cascade that he would most probably have pesented the precise immage of this one; nor could I for some time determine on which of those two great cataracts to bestoe the palm, on this or that which I had discovered yesterday; at length I determined between these two great rivals for glory that this was pleasingly beautifull, while the other was sublimely grand.

WEDNESDAY, JULY 6, 1994

We looked around Helena in the mid-afternoon, but our morning was spent on a boat tour through the Gates of the Mountains wilderness area. This area was given its name by William Clark due to opposing, rock cliffs, which seem to close like a gate when rounding a bend in the river.

We saw incredible rock formations and wildlife, including ospreys, bald eagles, pelicans and mountain goats. It was interesting to learn that most mountain goats die from falling from the rocky ledges for which they are so well adapted. After a dozen years or so, their teeth wear down to a point where they can no longer eat. Becoming weak, they often slip off the precipitous ledges that they have to negotiate.

Gates of the Mountains

In addition, we even saw a pictograph with information about a buffalo jump that was drawn on a limestone cliff wall with red paint by the Blackfeet Indians. This was an area where Blackfeet braves would perform the dangerous task of driving a herd of buffalo toward a cliff. One can imagine that these men had to be extremely careful not to become trampled by the stampeding animals that would unknowingly race to the edge of the cliff and plunge to their deaths. While this practice may seem brutal, it was a most efficient means of hunting. All of the buffalo remains were used for food, clothing and other purposes with little or no waste. One must keep in mind the immense numbers of animals in the herds that once roamed the West, and these buffalo jumps were a necessary part of the tribe's life. It was not until the white man began to develop the West that the continent witnessed a rapid decline in buffalo through their mass slaughter for sport, most of the carcasses left to waste and rot on the plains along the newly constructed railroad tracks.

Biking consisted of a short twenty-five miles from Helena to a point north of Townshend. One of the spokes on my rear wheel broke during the ride making this the third one to break between Todd and myself during our trip. This slowed us down considerably. It was at the finish point of this ride that we needed to have a meeting to address the way we were all feeling about various issues. Bob questioned the organization of the trip, and he was unsure about his responsibilities. Todd felt that we should be riding more. I felt that sufficient time needed to be taken to gather information. It was a very uncomfortable discussion to have with Todd, my partner and good friend, and Bob, my father-in-law. I am feeling responsible for this disagreement because I put the itinerary together and had unintentionally forced a change in our cycling plans by being sick for the past six days. As a result of our discussion, we agreed to make RV camps our destination points rather than towns. Also, since our communication devices do not always work, Bob will stay behind us and drive to predetermined meeting points to pick us up. This way, if we are behind schedule, he'll be able to find us and not worry about where we are. Things are a little tense. I miss Melina and want to see her very much. This is coloring the way I think and act, but I know that in two weeks I will finally see her. That will surely be one of the best days and happiest, fulfilling experiences that I can hope for.

Although it may seem at times as though things are out of control, I try to remind myself that everything has its purpose. While events may not be going according to "our" or "my" plan, I have to believe that they do have their place in the master scheme of life. There is a thread of continuity that can be traced between all life and its events. The trick is in trusting that the thread exists. There is a grand vision, and we play a tiny part in it. Like the image in a stained glass window, it is best viewed from afar and impossible to comprehend under a microscope. We must all have faith in ourselves and the forces which govern life. The trick is to simply look and wait. Strive to find the order within the chaos. In time, the solution to each perceived problem will be revealed.

MERIWETHER LEWIS – FRIDAY JULY 19TH 1805.

    . . . *this evening we entered much the most remarkable clifts that we have yet seen. these clifts rise from the waters edge on either side perpendicularly to the hight of 1200 feet. every object here wears a dark and gloomy aspect. the tow[er]ing and projecting rocks in many places seem ready to tumble on us. the river appears to have forced it's way through this immence body of solid rock for the distance of 5 3/4 Miles and where it makes it's exit below has th[r]own on either side vast columns of rocks mountains high.*

    the river appears to have woarn a passage just the width of it's channel or 150 yds. it is deep from side to side nor is there in the 1st 3 Miles of this distance a spot except one of a few yards in extent on which a man could rest the soal of his foot. several fine springs burst out at the waters edge from the interstices of the rocks. . . . it was late in the evening before I entered this place and was obliged to continue my rout untill sometime after dark before I found a place sufficiently large to encamp my small party; at length such an one occurred on the lard. side where we found plenty of lightwood and pich pine. this rock is a black granite below and appears to be of a much lighter colour above and from the fragments I take it to be flint of a yellowish brown and light creem-colored yellow. from the singular appearance of this place I called it the gates of the rocky mountains.

WILLIAM CLARK – JULY 21ST SUNDAY 1805

   a fine morning   our feet So brused and cut that I deturmined to delay for the Canoes, & if possible kill Some meet by the time they arrived,   Small birds are plenty. Some Deer, Elk, Goats, and Ibex; no buffalow in the Mountains. Those mountains are high and a great perportion of them rocky: Vallies firtile   I observe on the highest pinecals of some of the Mountains to the West Snow lying in Spots   Some Still Further North are covered with Snow and cant be Seen from this point

THURSDAY, JULY 7, 1994

First thing this morning I called Melina who, I was told on Wednesday evening, desperately wanted to talk to me. She was very happy to get the call, and I can't sufficiently say how good it feels to talk to her when I call home. After that, I called FHCDS and The Sports People. The Far Hills call was to get the number for a bike shop in Dillon, MT which turned out to be a hardware store that sold bikes. I talked to Priscilla and Jayne. Jayne was very happy to hear my voice and verify that I was OK. The Sports People call was to ask about spokes. We have collectively broken three spokes on the rear wheels of our bikes. We have two spare spokes left but have been replacing them in a real makeshift manner, and they look pretty mangled. The reason for this is that a rear spoke replacement means taking off the gear cluster, and we don't have the specific tools to do this. At this point it has become necessary to find a bike mechanic who can do it for us. The Sports People could not be sure why so many spokes were breaking, since a broken spoke is supposed to be a rarity. Since the Dillon "bike shop" was not a reliable source for a mechanic, we set our sights on Bozeman, MT as it was only about a thirty-minute drive from our campsite in Three Forks. I called the Summit

Bike Shop in Bozeman, explained our predicament and was told that we could bring our bikes in for immediate repair. That's exactly what we did. Forty-five minutes later we were in Bozeman. The owner said that the original spokes would continue to break under the stress of our ride. We ended up having both rear wheels respoked with top quality spokes and trued up as well. He also blew out our rubber handlebar grips so they wouldn't spin. Having arrived there at 10:30 A.M., we were told that the bikes would be finished by 2:00 P.M.

During the three-and-a-half hour wait, Todd, Bob and I explored the town of Bozeman, which turned out to be marvelous with great places to eat and shop in a college town/resort atmosphere. Todd seized the opportunity to purchase a pair of lizard skin cowboy boots that look pretty sharp on him. I continued my search for crumb cake which apparently does not exist west of the Mississippi. None to be had anywhere! Sandwiches and milkshakes were the fare for lunch, and we were able to pick up our bikes right on time. Bozeman is the kind of town where I could feel comfortable living. We had a great time, all due to broken spokes.

From Bozeman we drove to the Missouri Headwaters State Park in Three Forks, MT. We photographed the area where the Madison and Jefferson Rivers meet to form the Missouri River. This was a significant site for the Lewis and Clark expedition and proved to be a location which Sacagawea recognized from her childhood. Our last stop in the RV was a local museum in Three Forks which displayed all kinds of items from topics as diverse as Lewis and Clark to a barbed wire collection with 708 pieces! It's amazing what people collect!

At 4:30 P.M. we decided that we would ride to Lewis and Clark Caverns State Park and meet the RV there for the night. It was about a twenty-mile ride, but it gave us a chance to try out our newly spoked wheels. It also gave us our first glimpse of the Rocky Mountains that we were going to cross in two days! We had a beautiful ride with mountain views on three sides and a gentle, rolling road. There were no more broken spokes, so we are hoping that we have solved the problem; it was a maddening dilemma because they were breaking on level, paved roads without loaded panniers!

We got to Lewis and Clark Caverns State Park at 6:00 P.M. and took in the wonderful views. We were nestled in a little valley surrounded by mountains. There were great showers in the bathhouse, too. One begins to appreciate these civilized luxuries after a while. Bob was already fishing out on the Jefferson River when we arrived. Tomorrow we plan to ride from here to Dillon, MT. It will be our last night in Montana before crossing the Continental Divide! Earlier tonight I used the inspiration I feel in this area to do some writing.

Three Forks

Lives

All eyes of man, all eyes awake,
All lies upon each other break,
Go lift the veil upon the sea,
Go shatter mountains majesty

To fill the heart with parts unknown
To look beneath each unturned stone,
Fill up the void, let in the light,
Breathe in the air of darkest night,

Drink in the sounds where angels cry,
Reveal where mortal frailties lie,
Cast out the gods, demand their flight
And all that amortize your sight

For fate is loyal and time is dear,
And we've our lives to gather here,
And weave our lives together here.

Written at twilight in Lewis and Clark Caverns State Park, Montana, July 7, 1994

MERIWETHER LEWIS – SATURDAY JULY 27TH 1805 -

   . . . *at the distance of 3 3/4 Ms. further we arrived at 9. A.M. at the junction of the S.E. fork of the Missouri and the country opens suddonly to extensive and beatiful plains and meadows which appear to be surrounded in every direction with distant and lofty mountains; suposing this to be the three forks of the Missouri I halted the party on the Lard. shore for breakfast. and walked up the S.E. fork about 1/2 a mile and ascended the point of a high limestome clift from whence I commanded a most perfect view of the neighboring country. . . . believing this to be an essential part of the Continent I determined to remain at all events untill I obtained the necessary data for fixing it's latitude Longitude &c. . . .*

Friday, July 8, 1994

We began our ride at 7:30 A.M. and rode out of Lewis and Clark Caverns State Park. The first eight miles was through a gorgeous canyon. Then it opened up to farmland through the rest of the trip. Today's ride was seventy-five miles in length from Lewis and Clark Caverns to Dillon, Montana.

We stopped at a Jefferson Valley sign that reads: "Lewis and Clark expedition westward bound came up the Jefferson River in August 1805. They were hoping to find the Shoshoni Indians, Sacagawea's tribe, and trade for horses to use in crossing the mountains west of here. Just south of here the river forks; the east fork being the Ruby and the west fork being the Beaverhead. They followed the latter and met the Shoshoni. On their return trip from the coast in 1806, Captain William Clark retraced their former route down this valley to the Three Forks and then crossed to the Yellowstone. Captain Lewis left Clark at the Bitterroot Valley and crossed the divide, headed for Great Falls and met Clark at the confluence of the Missouri and the Yellowstone, arriving within nine days of each other."

A lunch of hickory burgers was had in Twin Bridges which is twenty-eight miles north of Dillon. Most of the ride was easy but stressful because of the trucks on the road and the narrow shoulder for riding. We have been told that truckers refer to cyclers as "road lice." We have not confirmed this report, but it makes us very cautious. We rode past Beaverhead Rock, another site recognized by Sacagawea in 1805 and one that was important to her people.

From the correct angle, and with a great deal of imagination, it can suggest the profile of a beaver's head. With the Native American culture being so closely in tune with the natural world, the resemblance would have been much more apparent that it is to people from today's modern society.

Dillon was the highlight of the day. We met the mayor, Jim Wilson, and found a GREAT bakery called Anna's Oven, which we plan to hit for breakfast buffet tomorrow. We befriended a woman named Kayleen who owns the flower store in town. We had stopped to ask about a good bakery and wound up talking about our trip. It turns out that she's a cyclist too. Later on, Kayleen ended up calling us at Anna's Oven to give us information on the Lemhi Pass about which she had made some phone calls. She was extremely helpful, and Todd and I gave her a Quest West T-shirt and a water bottle. Kayleen's efforts illustrate the

Beaverhead Rock – Do you see a beaver's head?

type of interest, response and assistance that we have experienced from many local individuals during our travels.

Bob caught a fifteen-inch brown trout today but bought shell steaks for dinner, as he releases all the fish he catches. We are looking forward to tomorrow's breakfast and our ride, which will bring us into Idaho and across the Continental Divide. I hope the roads are less traveled by trucks and that the mountains and trees are closer to the roads. I have become thoroughly tired of the Montana hills and farmland but try to appreciate each moment for its own rewards. Twelve days until reunion time!

We have had several "coincidental" events occur on our trip. It's interesting to note that the more I contemplate the idea of coincidences, the more I am convinced that they do not exist. If we look carefully with scrutiny and with awareness, we can begin to link the events in our lives with their cause and effect relationships. Even events that seem meaningless have a purpose. Understanding this allows for a view of ourselves and our actions in a new light. No longer are there insignificant acts. Every movement, every thought, every word has an impact on the present moment and those that will follow. A bird's wing will create a breeze, however slight. Ripples from a pebble tossed into the middle of a pond will eventually reach the shore. A kind word whispered in secret will benefit mankind. It's an exciting and rewarding challenge to remain continually aware and look for links between the events in life!

MERIWETHER LEWIS – THURSDAY AUGUST 8 1805.
    . . . the Indian woman recognized the point of a high plain to our right which she informed us was not very distant from the summer retreat of her nation on a river beyond the mountains which runs to the west. this hill she says her nation calls the beaver's head from a conceived re[s]emblance of it's figure to the head of that animal. . . .

SATURDAY, JULY 9, 1994

Today promised to be a hot day, 85° to 90°, but beautiful and sunny. We began with a wonderful breakfast buffet at Anna's Oven that offered waffles, French toast, eggs, fruit, sausage, biscuits & gravy, muffins and bacon. I had a Danish, French toast, a waffle and fruit. I intended to load up on carbohydrates but wanted to keep it light at the same time.

After breakfast we set off in the Rig for the Clark Canyon Reservoir because the interstate, which doesn't permit cycling, was the only route to get there. This leg of the trip is one that we have been anticipating for some time because it goes through Grant, Montana, over Lemhi Pass, across the Continental Divide and into Idaho.

The reservoir was beautiful. At the Camp Fortunate Overlook we saw an interpretive sign that reads: "Lewis and Clark expedition of 1804–1806 explored the upper reaches of the Louisiana Purchase to establish U.S. claims to the Pacific Northwest. Few points along their route have the significance of Camp Fortunate or Two Forks, now beneath the waters of Clark Canyon Reservoir. Captain Lewis, following an Indian trail in advance of the expedition's main party, first reached the junction of Red Rock River and Horse Prairie Creek on August 10, 1805. Two days later he crossed the Continental Divide at Lemhi Pass west of here and met Shoshoni Indians. On August 17th Lewis rejoined Clark and the main party at the site where they camped with the Shoshoni Indians until August 24th. After meeting, expedition interpreter Sacagawea, also a Shoshoni, was reunited with her brother Cameawaite whom she had not seen in five years. Through her, Lewis and Clark negotiated for horses, all important for the expedition's trip across the mountains to the Columbia River drainage. Here, too, expedition members cached canoes and supplies for their return. William Clark revisited this point in July of 1806 to empty the cache and begin the trip down the Missouri to Saint Louis. The camp bore the name Fortunate for meeting with the Indians and the important transition from water to overland travel. The actual valley where the reservoir is today they called 'Service Berry Valley' and Horse Prairie they designated 'Shoshoni Cove'."

We started riding at the Clark Canyon Dam, and while we had a bit of a climb in the beginning, we felt great. We stopped to take photographs of the Grant School because there is a big sign at the driveway that reads, "The 45 Parallel – Half way between the North Pole and the Equator." This was a surprise for us and an interesting point that we felt was worth noting.

We met the RV at the turnoff for Lemhi Pass and proceeded about fifteen miles on our bikes up a dirt and gravel road to the top of the Continental Divide, the point at which Lewis and Clark first left the Louisiana Purchase territory. Heading up Lemhi Pass road we saw our first herd of pronghorn antelope, seven of them. We stopped for a water break, and six of the seven took off. One was just sort of checking us out. Pretty cool! The pronghorn antelope is supposed to be one of the fastest land animals, second only to the cheetah.

In addition to the spectacular beauty of the surrounding mountains, much of the winding, dirt road that we were following was lined with gorgeous wild-flowers such as Indian Paintbrush and Lupine.

On the way up we passed a wonderful ranch called the Bar Double T (-TT). Excellent spot . . . Todd wants to move there! We were not challenged as much as we had

45ᵗʰ Parallel

expected by this leg of the journey, but our rewards were incredible. What a view!

There were mountains as far as I could see, and I could not help but think of the disappointment that the Lewis and Clark expedition must have felt at this spot. They had expected that they might be able to see an easy water route to the Pacific Ocean, the much hoped for Northwest Passage! I can only hope that the beauty of this Lemhi Pass area was not lost in their frustration.

The ride down the other side (thirteen miles to Tendoy, Idaho) was much steeper, and our hands began to ache from the continual braking we had to do. On the way down we saw a moose in a small pool of water. They are as big as horses! Just as we finished looking at the moose, it started to thunder and lightning. We rode through it and were only dampened by a few showers. At the bottom, we faced a twenty-one-mile ride on paved roads to Salmon, Idaho where we spent the night. Again, we had a situation where we could have been caught in heavy rain, but God has smiled upon us. This was one of the best days we have had and my favorite to date. The Continental Divide was incredible! I feel much more secure amidst the mountains and the trees; we're not as exposed as on the plains. Tomorrow we head into Montana again.

I tried to call home several times today, but no one was home. I'll try early tomorrow morning. I want to share my excitement! Seventy miles were covered today.

view of Montana looking down from Lemhi Pass

Gordon and Todd at Lemhi Pass

view of Idaho from Lemhi Pass

MERIWETHER LEWIS – MONDAY AUGUST 12, 1805.

    . . . at the distance of 4 miles further the road took us to the most distant fountain of the waters of the Mighty Missouri in surch of which we have spent so many toilsome days and wristless nights. thus far I had accomplished one of those great objects on which my mind has been inalterably fixed for many years, judge then of the pleasure I felt in all[a]ying my thirst with this pure and ice-cold water which issues from the base of a low mountain or hill of a gentle ascent for 1/2 a mile. the mountains are high on either hand leave this gap at the head of this rivulet through which the road passes. here I halted a few minutes and rested myself. two miles below McNeal had exultingly stood with a foot on each side of this little rivulet and thanked his god that he had lived to bestride the mighty & heretofore deemed endless Missouri. after refreshing ourselves we proceeded on to the top of the dividing ridge from which I discovered immence ranges of high mountains still to the West of us with their tops partially covered with snow. I now descended the mountain about 3/4 of a mile which I found much steeper than on the opposite side, to a handsome bold runing Creek of cold Clear water.

Todd and I headed out of Salmon, Idaho this morning and traveled north on route 93. We had a slight headwind, but the trip into North Fork was downhill following the Salmon River. Wonderful rock formations can be found along this stretch of the road. We stopped in North Fork for a snack and a drink at the General Store. We also stopped in the Lewis and Clark Cafe just south of Gibbonsville. With a name like this we couldn't resist. They have excellent apple pie and strawberry pie. From here we continued our ride to Gibbonsville where we had to put our bikes on the RV. The road construction at Lost Trail Pass prevented any bike riding from Gibbonsville, Idaho to Sula, Montana.

We got back on our bikes in Sula and picked Hamilton, MT as our destination. The road started off as beautiful as it could be with steep slopes on either side and the Bitterroot River winding along the road. The slopes were covered in the dark green of evergreen trees. One of the towns that we passed through, Darby, was a place we decided to stop. Darby is a very clean town, and one in which we both felt very comfortable. We stopped in a trendy coffee shop with a dining porch where we sat and took in some of the local comings and going of the people. This proved to be a calming and rejuvenating break before resuming our trek. Todd especially liked this town, and it was dubbed as "another place we could live."

The remainder of our ride gave us views of the Bitterroot peaks, some of which still had snow on them.

We passed a man driving a tractor who comically, I think, said that he was driving from Alaska. We finally got to Anglers Roost RV Camp. All of us are in high spirits and very satisfied with today's ride. We made phone calls to Kris and Melina, my mother and Todd's parents and settled in for our evening's dinner of chicken and rice. Melina also called me before she went to bed. It was the best way to end the day for her and me. Unfortunately, the bathrooms are out of order here, so we will be heading out tomorrow morning as soon as possible.

Our awakening in the Anglers Roost this morning was accompanied by the prospect of no showers and no toilets due to a septic problem at the campground. As it turned, out the problem was remedied enough to allow us to shower before we went into Hamilton. We had a short ride ahead of us today, so we knew that we could spend some time during the morning investigating and exploring around town, which we did. We drove into Hamilton at 9:00 A.M. and had breakfast at a busy place called the Coffee Cup. Bob had a huge sticky bun, Todd had two eggs, hash browns, toast and orange juice, and I had two, whole wheat pancakes and a quarter melon. After breakfast I went into a Safeway and bought sunscreen; it's essential when riding.

Instead of riding up Route 93, which had a good deal of truck traffic, it was decided to take local roads 269 and 203 to the west, which paralleled Route 93 up to Florence. Twenty miles brought us to Stevensville, and Todd and I stopped in a cute, little coffee shop for a snack to keep our energy levels high. I was glad to be riding off of the main road. The secondary roads meandered through farmland, allowed us to relax, and most likely provided better views. Another twelve miles brought us out in Florence and onto Rt. 93. It was nine miles from Florence to Lolo where we had planned to meet the Rig between 1:30 and 2:00 P.M.

We passed Travelers Rest, a camping site for Lewis and Clark, and got to Lolo at 1:45 P.M. There was no sign of Bob or the Rig, so we stopped in at the Lolo Cafe to look at the menu. It looked like a good place to eat lunch, but our main priority was meeting the RV. We went back to the intersection of Rt. 93 and Rt. 12 and waited. At approximately 2:20 P.M., Bob showed up in the Rig after having a very successful morning of fishing – three brook trout. Todd and I loaded the bikes on the rack and noted that this officially marked the transition point in our journey from bicycles to frame packs. I drove us to the Lolo Cafe for a light lunch. From there, we got into the Rig and headed for Missoula which was eleven-miles north of Lolo.

It is interesting to note that not much conversation takes place between Todd and myself during the day. While we may have conversations during breaks, the only verbal communication we have is when we pass each other to take turns being the lead rider. Our single file riding formation and the traffic noise diminishes the amount of talking we can do, but the biggest factor that inhibits conversation is the wind noise in our ears as we ride; at times it can drown out everything else, especially when riding into a headwind. Todd and I have both remarked about the irony of spending so much of our days riding only a few feet apart but having so little time to talk.

Our campsite for the night was the KOA campground to the northeast of town . . . close to the airport and convenient to the center of Missoula. Since I had been craving pizza, we ordered a mushroom and sausage pie from a place in town that delivered. A half hour later we were eating. Excellent! We also ate a number of fudge stripe cookies (A.K.A. Stripers) that had become a staple on our trip. We are indebted to Bob for his suggestion to buy the first of many packages back in Bismarck.

After dinner, I went for a short ride to explore the immediate area around the campground. We will probably turn in early tonight due to Bob's early flight tomorrow morning at 8:40 A.M. Todd and I also want to get an early start, so we can get some information and make some firm and final decisions about our Lolo Trail backpack.

The highlight of the afternoon/evening was when Melina called our RV cellular phone just to say "hi." We miss each other very much and are both counting the days until her arrival. Nine days to go!

P.S. A male peacock with long, colorful tail feathers strutted by the RV tonight.

Bitterroot peak with snow

MERIWETHER LEWIS – MONDAY SEPTEMBER 9TH 1805.

 . . . *we continued our rout down the W. side of the river about 5 miles further and encamped on a large creek which falls in on the West. as our guide inform me that we should leave the river at this place and the weather appearing settled and fair I determined to halt the next day rest our horses and take som scelestial Observations. we called this Creek Travellers rest.*

TUESDAY, JULY 12, 1994

Today was an organizational and restructuring day. It began with a trip to the Missoula airport at 7:30 A.M. Bob flew home today on an 8:40 A.M. flight, and we all had a breakfast of pancakes and French toast in the airport restaurant before he left.

After Bob departed, Todd and I made some telephone calls. I called the Portland, OR radio station, and Todd checked in with the Somerset Hills Answering Service and Josh Balling from the Hills-Bedminster Press. I also called school. It seems that the Bradburys, a family we know from New Jersey, are going to arrange a rafting trip for us on the Salmon River after our Lolo backpack. It will be the perfect place in our itinerary for that kind of diversion. I'm even more excited because our families will be here to share the experience with us.

We drove the Rig to the Lolo Pass Visitor Information Center to try and get information and advice on our backpack route, but the man to which we spoke suggested that we talk to someone at the Powell Ranger Station, about which Todd and I had heard good things. We headed down there and were not disappointed. We were helped by Cheri (pronounced "cherry") Jones who told us what we needed to hear. She was a wealth of knowledge and really helped us plot out where we wanted to get on the trail and where we wanted to get off. When we finished, it was decided that we would more or less follow the Lolo Trail, also known as Forest Service Road 500. The Lewis and Clark Trail weaves above and below the Lolo Trail, a historic Nez Perce Indian trade and hunting route across the Bitterroot Mountains to the Clearwater River, and is not yet cut. We would access the trail via the Wendover Ridge Trail and get off at the Lochsa Historical Ranger Station.

There are three options open to us at the conclusion of our hike, which gives us the ability to use the available time to our best advantage. Our first option is to come directly down to the Historical Station via Forest Service Road 107, or for our second option, we can continue our backpack on the Lolo Trail a bit further, backtrack and come down on 107. The third option open to us would be to go a little bit further on the Lolo Trail and then come down on Forest Service Road 101 which would take us quite a bit further west. Due to our variety of options, we will see how much time we have at our disposal when we get to the intersection of 500 and 107 and make our decision at that point.

Before returning to Missoula, we stood in front of the Powell Ranger Station at a place on the Lewis and Clark Trail called Colt Killed Creek.

This is the location where Lewis and Clark needed to kill a colt for food as they were crossing the Bitterroot Mountains. It's a beautiful river, the Lochsa River, that runs through here . . . real tall lodgepole pines. It's just a great place. Feeling satisfied and confident about our backpack, we took a few photographs, shot some video and headed back to Missoula where we returned to the KOA campground in Missoula (about 50 miles away) to check in for the day and evening. I also need to find a place to get some boot laces and a thermal mattress for the hike.

The rest of the day was spent organizing. Todd cleaned the Rig, and I made reservations for Kris and Melina in Missoula and called the RV repair shop, also in Missoula. Not only will they service the Rig in time for Kris to pick it up, they will also meet her at the airport. In addition, Phyllis from the RV shop agreed to drive Todd, Susie and me to the trailhead on Friday morning and then drive our RV back to their place for servicing. What nice people! We also need to remember to pick up the inner tubes on Friday morning, which were sent from The Sports People in NJ to the RV shop in Missoula, MT.

The evening was spent planning the camping sites for the September, 1994, Far Hills Country Day School Northern Experience. Todd and I plan this trip every year for the

Colt Killed Creek

School, and there is a permit request letter that I need to send tomorrow to a ranger in the Adirondack Mountains.

Melina called me again today. It was fulfilling to speak with her, but it makes me depressed. I am also envious of Bob who is going to have Melina overnight tomorrow. The reunion that we will have at the Lochsa Historical Ranger Station is going to be spectacular and long-awaited.

I feel as if I might be getting a cold. I can not believe how sick I've been on this trip. If the congestion and cough do not subside overnight, I'll start taking Comtrex tomorrow. I need to be healthy for our backpack departure on Friday! I've learned that Kris has strep throat and Melina is having trouble sleeping. This trip seems to be adversely affecting all three of us in different ways.

WILLIAM CLARK – SEPTEMBER 14TH THURSDAY (SATURDAY) 1805
   . . . *we proceeded on 2 miles & Encamped opposit a Small Island at the mouth of a branch on the right side of the river which is at this place 80 yards wide, Swift and Stoney,   here we were compelled to kill a Colt for our men & Selves to eat for the want of meat & we named the South fork Colt killed Creek, . . .*

Wednesday, July 13, 1994

Well, another exciting day on the Ponderosa! Not exactly, but we managed to occupy our time rather well. Breakfast occurred on The Rig, and then we took our bikes into town. We had heard that there was a gathering in Caras Park in Missoula called "Out to Lunch." Basically, most of the restaurants set up booths in the park with food from 11:00 A.M. until 1:30 P.M., and there is entertainment under a tent in the center of all the action. We sat on the grass, ate well and enjoyed an acoustic guitarist/singer and a follies quartet.

After lunch I purchased a new air mattress for the backpacking trip because my old one no longer held air. The salesperson was a guy that roomed with a FHCDS graduate in college! I also had my camera checked out because it was occasionally rewinding film before the roll was finished. Todd and I split up in town. He went to buy mini audio cassettes, and I went to check out the room that I reserved for Kris and Melina.

The late afternoon and evening was spent reviewing Northern Experience plans, discussing our Lolo backpack, doing laundry and scavenging for food. Seven days until my family leaves to join us in Idaho.

Plans were also made with Exodus, the Bradbury's rafting company, for our trip. Looks like we're going down on the evening of the twenty-first, staying in the lodge and then going rafting on the twenty-second. It promises to be a great place for a reunion and an exciting and fun activity for everyone!

Right now I'm eating a strawberry Pop-Tart. We've got tons of these things that we are consuming out of boredom. It's more difficult than you might imagine to stick to a healthy, well balanced diet when you're on the road. Susie comes in tomorrow at 12:00 P.M., and we'll get stuff packed up so that we can leave on Friday. I have a cold, so at some point I have to get some cold medicine . . . Comtrex or something like that. We were supposed to get rain showers in the afternoon, but we never got any. The weather's been quite cooperative. I hope it holds for Lolo. Anyway, I guess that's about it. I'll watch a little tube and hit the sack. Tomorrow will go quickly with Susie arriving at the airport, packing and doing our last minute planning. So, that's it for now. I'll write more tomorrow.

THURSDAY, JULY 14, 1994

The separation from my family is continuing to cause anxiety for me. Susie flew into Missoula today and had a much deserved and anticipated reunion with Todd. It was great to see them so happy, but it made the yearning to see my family all the more intense. Tomorrow will bring our first day of backpacking and the last time that I will be able to call home for a week. However, next Thursday, July 21st, will be my day for reunion, as we plan to meet at the Lochsa Historical Ranger Station at 1:00 P.M. I have a feeling that the time on the trail will pass quickly.

We spent today organizing our frame packs for tomorrow's departure. A late lunch (3:00 P.M.) was had in a 1950s-style diner in Missoula, and we treated ourselves to lodging at the 4 B's Inn in Missoula. A good night's sleep was agreed to be important, seeing as we will be spending the next six days and nights sleeping in a tent and backpacking on the Lolo Trail. This should be one of the more exciting segments of the trip. We are eager to experience the Lolo Trail and have spent a great deal of time and energy insuring the safest and most organized approach possible. In short, I am looking forward to savoring the experience and the fruits of our investigations and planning, but the reward of reunion at the conclusion of the backpack is now my ultimate goal and incentive.

Part 4

The Lolo Trail

Yesterday was our first day on the Lolo Trail. It started with a huge breakfast in, of all places, the Missoula airport. We had had a great breakfast there on Tuesday and figured that it was very near the RV repair center where we needed to bring our Rig. Phyllis Pettijohn drove Todd, Susie and me in her pickup truck into the Bitterroot Mountains to the beginning of the Wendover Ridge Trail. It is located just three miles west of the Powell Ranger Station on Route 12 in Idaho. We filled up our two water bottles each and headed out. We did ask the campground host about the trail. He told us that the top of the trail was difficult to follow, but if we kept heading north along the ridge, we would be fine. We walked across Route 12 and started up the Wendover Ridge Trail. It was poorly marked, but the trail was well worn and easily followed. However, the trail was very steep with a 3,200-ft. increase in elevation and a relentless climb shrouded in dense red spruce and lodgepole pine. We found ourselves thankful that we had our water, always keeping an eye out for the streams and rivulets that were indicated on the map for pumping additional water.

We soon reached a logging road and followed the trail across the road after Todd treated blisters on the backs of his heels. Still the trail climbed, and we eventually approached the intersection with an even older logging road, now overgrown, where we were told it was easy to lose the trail. We did. The first path that we took led to a dead end, at a cliff, and the second, although affording us spectacular views, began to lead off the ridge. Remembering that the trail followed the ridge line, I eventually found the Wendover Ridge Trail by dropping my pack and bushwhacking up toward the crest of the ridge.

After we all got back on the trail, we decided to rest at a clear, level spot for lunch. We were all tired and wanted to pass the Lewis and Clark Wendover Ridge Rest Site, as this marked the halfway point on the trail. After about thirty minutes, we continued our hike. It was very hot, we were short on water and miserable from the steep climb. It would seem that the streams indicated on our map are seasonal, as we found no rivulets or streams at all. On September 15, 1805, William Clark noted a similar difficulty in finding water after his climb up Wendover Ridge and had to melt the snow they found at the top. There was one point where I considered going back since we were half way through our water supply, the heat continued to build and there wasn't a hint of another water source anywhere. Todd's

Lolo Trail

legs were shaking, and Susie and I were feeling weak. We knew that if we continued to head north, eventually we would have to cross the Lolo Trail, dirt road number 500. The trail seemed to stretch on and up forever, we hadn't passed the Rest Site, which was supposed to be marked, and we were feeling frustrated, weak and worried about our health and supply of water. We were already dehydrated. Little did we know that our lunch site was the Lewis and Clark Wendover Ridge Rest Site. It would seem that the same moderation in grade, which persuaded the famous explorers to choose this as a resting site, had the same influence on the three of us.

The uphill battle continued. Suddenly Susie spotted a small wooden sign, and I saw the rough, dirt road, the Lolo Trail! We rejoiced at the knowledge that we were finally off the Wendover Ridge Trail. Actually we were quite giddy, and I felt good about being able to pinpoint our location on the map. Still, we knew that we had to find water – and quickly!

Then something amazing happened. Todd and I had already run into a situation where we encountered an "angel" above Fort Peck Lake in the form of a road-grader driver. Now it was something else. Understand that only three cars or so, on the average, are said to travel along the Lolo Trail per day. Unbelievably, just as we had dropped our packs, a car appeared over the crest of the hill to the east. The car slowed and then stopped in front of us. We were in the middle of asking if they had passed or noticed any water source when the man and woman in the car said there was none. While disturbing, this news saved us a trip since we had planned to split up in order to find a source of water. One was to go east, the others west. The really miraculous part happened next. The couple said we looked thirsty and proceeded to give us an entire water bottle full of it. Then they verified that there was a good spring, a water source, three miles west. After thanking them, they simply drove slowly out of sight. "What are the chances of that occurring?," we asked ourselves. "Were these two individuals people or angels? Was this meeting chance, circumstance or fate?"

view near Wendover Ridge

Whichever was the case, we definitely felt that there was a higher power watching out for us on this trip.

After partially satisfying our thirst, we put our backpacks on and headed down the road. Sure enough, we passed a stream in about three miles – clear and cold water and plenty of it. We filled our water bottles, pushed liquids by drinking a quart each and refilled those bottles.

By now it was 6:00 P.M., and we needed to find a campsite. All of the land was sloped, so it was hard to find a suitable location. Our feet hurt, and we were hoping to find one soon. I imagine we walked about one and a half miles further, and I finally spotted a place up off the right side of the road. That was it. We set up camp and ate noodles and chicken with mixed vegetables out on a rocky point overlooking the surrounding mountains and forest. What a spectacular sight!

After hanging our food, we all crawled into the tent for a well deserved night's sleep. During the night, we were awakened by three distinct events. The first was the sound of a deer or elk running down the dirt road beneath us. The second was the sound of a man, somewhere in the distance around midnight, screaming "hey!" a dozen or so times. This was followed, about twenty minutes later, by a truck that drove down the motorway. I was glad to be up above the road where our tent could not be seen. The last interruption was the sound of a deer's warning signal, sounding much like a loud cough, below us in the forest. After sleeping on and off, I awoke and got up at 5:30 A.M. on Saturday, July 16. It was going to be another sunny day. Four days 'till Kris and Melina leave New Jersey.

WILLIAM CLARK – SEPTEMBER 12TH THURSDAY 1805.

The road through this hilley Country is verry bad passing over hills & thro' Steep hollows, over falling timber &c. &c. continued on & passed Some most intolerable road on the Sides of the Steep Stoney mountains, which might be avoided by keeping up the Creek which is thickly covered with under groth & falling timber. Crossed a Mountain 8 miles with out water & encamped on a hill side on the Creek after Decending a long Steep mountain, Some of our Party did not get up untill 10 oClock PM. Party and horses much fatigued.

WILLIAM CLARK – WEDNESDAY (SUNDAY) SEPTR. 15TH 1805

proceeded on Down the right Side of (koos koos kee) River over Steep points Rocky & buschey as usial for 4 miles to an old Indian fishing place, here the road leaves the river to the left and assends a mountain winding in every direction to get up the Steep assents & to pass the emence quantity of falling timber which had [been] falling from dift. causes i e fire & wind and has deprived the greater part of the Southerly Sides of this mountain of its green timber, Several horses Sliped and roled down Steep hills which hurt them verry much the one which Carried my desk & Small trunk Turned over & roled down a mountain for 40 yards & lodged against a tree, broke the Desk the horse escaped and appeared but little hurt after two hours delay we proceeded on up the mountain Steep & ruged as usial, more timber near the top, when we arrived at the top As we Conceved, we could find no water and Concluded to Camp and make use of the Snow we found on the top to cook the remns. of our Colt & make our Supe, evening verry cold and cloudy. Two of our horses gave out, pore and too much hurt to proceed on and left in the rear. nothing killed to day except 2 Phests.

From this mountain I could observe high ruged mountains in every direction as far as I could see.

SATURDAY, JULY 16, 1994

After finishing yesterday's journal entry this morning, we had a breakfast of freeze dried blueberry pancakes and sausage and instant oatmeal. It wasn't what you would expect from a restaurant, but it served its purpose. We packed up and went back up the trail to a spring that we had passed the day before. Since we don't know what lies ahead in terms of water, it was decided that we had better fill up before leaving.

The hiking was very slow today. We left at 9:45 A.M. in bright sunshine. Our feet hurt and Todd's blisters were bad. Our hips were also uncomfortable from the hip belts of our frame packs. We covered about seven miles today, half of which were uphill. We passed no water, so we were thankful that we had filled our bottles in the morning. While backpacking, our attention was

view from the Lolo Trail

totally focused on listening for the sound of running water. Sometimes we would be fooled by the sound of the wind in the tops of the trees, but mostly it was silent . . . a silence broken only by our rhythmic footsteps and the occasional cry of a raven, chickadee or jay.

Eventually we came to a spot named that Lewis and Clark had named Bear Oil and Roots. The site was named after the ingredients of a meal that the explorers had here while they camped on June 27, 1806. As we came to expect, there was no sign, but there were two signposts where a sign was intended to be installed. We have found these trails and sites to be extremely poorly marked, but I understand that there is an effort to install signage on the entire trail in time for the 200th anniversary of the Lewis and Clark expedition. The good part about this site was that there was a spring that ran out of a drainage pipe at the edge of the road. All of us drank a full bottle of water and refilled all of our bottles.

As it was 2:00 P.M., it was decided that we should stay at this location for the night. This place gave us water for cooking, and we also took this opportunity to wash ourselves and our dirty laundry. We had no soap, but a rinsing was better than nothing and felt refreshing.

I climbed the ridge next to the road and saw the most wonderful panorama of the surrounding mountains . . . ridge line after ridge line greying off into the distance. What a sense of freedom we had! On the top of our ridge was a meadow, and all around me lay a carpet of purple, blue, yellow, white and scarlet wildflowers that were stirring with the activity of several species of colorful butterflies. We were fortunate to witness such a dazzling display.

Todd and Susie joined me on the ridge to experience the rewarding panorama and said that they had found a terrific campsite around the bend in the road. We wasted no time in moving our packs to the site. It was great, secluded under trees yet accessible to the Lolo Trail and water, and while Todd and Susie put up the tent, I chose a spot for hanging food and strung the necessary rope. Todd and Susie decided to nap for a while, and I sat on my foam pad and eventually napped in the sun on the point in front of our campsite. Dinner was at 6:00 P.M., about thirty minutes after we woke. Pasta Roma, peas and ice cream (all freeze dried) was the choice.

While I was hanging the food after dinner, I noticed a most interesting sight. There on the top of the ridge where I had seen all the butterflies was the form of a woman cloaked in robes. The figure had to be at least twenty-five feet tall, and it startled me when I first saw it. After continued scrutiny and inspection, it proved to be a dead tree trunk, but for some unknown reason my first impression was that it reminded me of those visions of Mary that people have claimed to see from time to time. Although I am a Christian, this struck me as unusual because I am not Catholic, nor can I say that I have any strong ties to any one particular Christian doctrine or denomination. Still, this image stuck in my mind and impressed me as being a link to those times that we have had of feeling protected and cared for by a higher power. I now believe more than ever that we have an unseen partner on this expedition.

Having had this experience, I find it amazing that I had so quickly created a religious image out of the form of a dead tree. What made my mind operate in this manner? Was it based on imagery that was ingrained into my brain as a child? Was it a random association, or was I maneuvered into the correct line of sight and influenced by a greater force? I know that I would not be writing these words were it not for the powerful visual impact from this experience. We have spent much of our time worrying, despite the fact that we have had reminders along our journey that suggested we were being assisted and protected. I guess someone or something wanted to make sure I got the point. Well, it worked!

This whole imagery issue has me deep in thought. What does our Creator look like? Why do we look the way we do? Some beliefs state that man was created in God's image, and I use the word "God" with no specific, religious or denominational reference. If so, does it mean that we, therefore, resemble God in physical appearance? If one ponders the human body, it is interesting to note how this incredible machine is perfectly adapted to our life . . . on earth. Every part and physical quality of the body, our height, weight, arms, legs, mouths, skin color, fingers, sexual organs, etc., is designed to maintain our existence and reproduction on this planet. But what need of existence on this specific planet, or any other for that matter, might an omnipotent, creative entity have? If God is infinite, universal and everlasting, then the part of us that is in the likeness of God must have the same qualities. Looking inward to the intangible, one sees that the soul, our spirit, is the only part of us not bound to the laws of nature, as we understand them to be. It may be more correct to say that we are created in God's spiritual image. Our feelings, capacity for compassion, trust, faith, love and empathy are our infinite qualities and our direct link with the power and essence of the Creator. We would do well to look to them for guidance more often.

The reverse would also apply. Since we assume that God is a spiritual force, everlasting, infinite and universal, there would be no need for a physical body which is limiting through its specialization. Perhaps spiritual entities, angels and the like take human form only to be understood by men and women. In this manner, people may more easily accept the presence of God, and God can work in the intangible.

Given our acceptance of a universal creative force, what might be the nature of our relationship with it? Does it renew itself? Most of us at one point have heard of and studied the water system. It's a closed system which operates on its own. Water falls from clouds as raindrops. The rain runs off of the land into rivers, seas and oceans. Water evaporates into the air and eventually condenses as water vapor to form clouds, which will, in turn, provide more rain. This cycle occurs continually and can teach us much about that which is eternal in us. If part of the Creator or God, call it what you may, is in us, then we are part of a greater power. To know the Creator we can look inside ourselves. Just as a raindrop shares similarities with the ocean or the cloud from which it came, so do we carry an essence with us that is like God, only smaller. In keeping with this analogy, as individuals we may be more like snowflakes, each having differences yet fundamentally identical in composition. Eventually, we will return to the great pool from which we came and come to share the full peace and knowledge of this Force. We study the small to understand the large. Similarly, we should look within ourselves to begin to know God.

Having philosophized for some length, let me return to this evening's events and plans. After dinner, Todd, Susie and I got more water and settled in for the evening. We are excited by the trail, as far as Lewis and Clark sites are concerned, but we are finding the lack of water to be disturbing, even dangerous. This has made us have a change of plans, and we plan to be off the trail and back on Route 12 in two days. Our new plan is to hike to Howard Camp tomorrow because we know it has water. From there we will take Road #107 down to Route 12 where we will camp for the remaining two and a half days while we wait for Kristen and Melina. Susie is finding the isolation slightly frightening, Todd's heels are in bad shape, and I am concerned about our health and safety. We should all feel better when we are off the Lolo Trail and Thursday arrives.

WILLIAM CLARK – FRIDAY JUNE 27TH 1806
. . . we continued our march and . . . here we Encamped for the night . . . our Meat being exhosted we issued a point of Bears Oil to a mess which with their boiled roots made an agreeable dish. . . .

SUNDAY, JULY 17, 1994

Today we backpacked approximately eight miles from Bear Oil and Roots to Howard Camp. The going was largely uphill, and in some places it was rather steep. About five miles into the trip, we stopped at Indian Post Office. Our day started at 7:45 A.M. when we hit the trail, and we arrived at Howard Camp at 1:45 P.M. Having been awakened by the warning signals of a large buck this morning, we were on the lookout for other deer along the way.

We arrived at Indian Post Office at 10:30 A.M. It's a beautiful spot that overlooks the surrounding mountains, and it is the highest point on the Lolo Trail at 7,033 feet. Cairns, originally placed by Indians to help guide the way, are seen every eighty yards or so. This site got its name from the idea that Native Americans supposedly would leave messages for each other inside the rock cairns. Lewis and Clark noted a similar cairn located farther to the west on their return journey in 1806. While we were on top of Indian Post Office, I placed a rock on top of a cairn for Melina.

We even got a photograph of it. Todd and Susie each placed a rock on the cairn as well.

Todd's feet were bothering him a great deal today, and we are all very weary from the hike, heat and water conservation that we are forced to endure. A bright spot in today's hike was a lunch stop about a mile from Howard Camp. We were in a very light-hearted mood and were grateful to have peanut butter and jelly to eat. Susie even said, "I am so contented," as we lay on the dirt road resting our feet with flies buzzing around us after lunch.

After we arrived at Howard Camp, our priorities were to pump water at a nearby stream and establish a campsite. While exploring the surrounding area, I spotted a mother partridge hen and about eight chicks. I was surprised at the fact that they did not try to escape me.

Still, at present, the historical/landmark signs leave much to be desired. None of the Lewis and Clark sights have been marked, and the only way we can find them is by using our mapping skills. As mentioned, some of the sites have posts but no signs. Tomorrow we plan to do a nine mile hike to Route 12. If we are successful, we can camp along the Lochsa River for the next three nights as we make our way to the Lochsa Historical Ranger Station. There is a chance that we might be able to telephone Kris and arrange an earlier pickup before she and Melina leave. Having watched the change in Todd, I am anticipating my own renaissance when they arrive.

WILLIAM CLARK – FRIDAY JUNE 27TH 1806

the road Still continue[d] on the hights of the Dividing ridge on which we had traveled yesterday for 9 Ms. or to our encampment of the 16th Septr. last. about 1 M. short of the encampment we halted by the request of the Guides a fiew minits on an ellevated point and smoked a pipe   on this eminance the nativs have raised a conic mound of Stons of 6 or 8 feet high and erected a pine pole of 15 feet long. from this place we had an extencive view of these Stupendeous Mountains principally covered with snow like that on which we stood; we were entirely serounded by those mountains from which to one unacquainted with them it would have Seemed impossible ever to have escaped, in short without the assistance of our guides, I doubt much whether we who had once passed them could find our way to Travelers rest in their present situation for the marked trees on which we had placed considerable reliance are much fewer and more difficuelt to find than we had apprehended. . . .

Melina's rock on top of the Indian Post Office cairn

MONDAY, JULY 18, 1994

The clouds made an attempt to threaten our good weather, but the sun eventually won out. Our backpack today took us four miles to the junction of 500 and 107. We never saw Devil's Chair, a large, natural rock formation, because there were no signs or trails visible to us as we hiked toward 107. Disappointed, but not surprised at the lack of signage and directions for historical sites and points of interest, we started our descent on 107, a dirt road. A road sign at the junction indicated that it was nine miles to Route 12. Bracing ourselves for the strain of the long downhill hike, during which we would descend 3,600 feet, we left the Lolo Trail and headed for Route 12 and, we thought, a telephone.

The hike down on 107 consisted of mostly switchbacks, and our toes ached from the continual jamming of our toes into the front of our boots. Todd did not want to stop because of his blistered heels; the sooner we reached the bottom, the sooner the boots could come off.

Susie has kept our minds occupied during much of our backpacking over the past few days by keeping us engaged in some interesting conversations. They were great fun and ranged from serious talks about marriage, honesty and commitment to lighter and sillier topics such as our favorite foods, movies, etc. Her energy seemed to make some of the more difficult times pass much faster.

Finally, the Lochsa River and Route 12 came into view, although the mile markers indicated that there were four miles to go. They were the longest four miles I've ever hiked, but eventually we rounded a bend in the road, and Route 12 lay before us.

We walked across the two lane road, which curved out of site in both directions, and we headed down a dirt trail where we had lunch and used the opportunity to remove our boots. A campsite and a phone were our next priorities. We thought that if we could make it to the Lochsa Historical Ranger Station, our prearranged pick-up point, I could call Kris and tell her that we were out early. The only problem was that the Ranger Station was eighteen miles west of our present location. After searching the area for suitable campsites, we decided to try and find a ride west to the Lochsa Historical Ranger Station. It was 2:00 P.M. at this point.

Finding no one to ask for a ride, we did the next best thing; we hitched. This seemed uncomfortable to me, since I would never dream of doing this in New Jersey, but somehow in the middle of a forest in Idaho it seemed safe, especially since all three of us were together. We must have presented a pretty disheveled sight for passing motorists, of which there were

weary feet on the Lolo Trail

precious few. To make a long story short, we stood, sat and lay on the side of the road for one and a half hours. Todd took photos of Susie and I with our thumbs out as he lay in the weeds on the opposite side of the road.

The people that did come down the road passed and waved, and one person turned his car around at our intersection of 107 and 12.

Finally a small, blue car coming east, opposite from the direction we wanted to go, pulled over, and a young woman named Erin asked if we needed a ride. Enthusiastic, we said that we needed to go to the ranger station, and she invited us to pack ourselves and our packs into her compact car. It seems that Erin had passed us once and decided to turn around, come back and offer us a ride. I sat in front holding Erin's computer, and Todd and Susie sat in the back seat with both of our packs on their laps. Susie's pack managed to fit into the trunk. Amidst our packs and Erin's belongings, we settled in, as she turned her car around and headed west on Route 12.

Fast does not accurately describe Erin's driving, and all of us wished, hoped and prayed that we would make it in one piece. Route 12 is a very winding, rather narrow highway that follows the Lochsa River. With this in mind you can understand my (our) distress at Erin's

looking for a ride to the Lochsa Historical Ranger Station

fondness for pushing the speed on curves and passing, with a limited view, semi trucks that were transporting logs. Erin, however, seemed very calm as she told us that she used to work in Lolo and that she was presently on her way home to Lewiston, Idaho from college in Denver. She was also involved in looking into graduate programs in psychology. As if the ride were not exciting enough, Erin popped in a Counting Crows tape which seemed to fuel her confidence in driving the snake-like road. I confess that I had to put my sunglasses on to hide the fear in my eyes. Finally the ranger station came into view, and we thankfully unloaded ourselves and our packs. Erin gave us her address and phone number and invited us to stop in when we reached Lewiston, Idaho. We were very grateful for the ride but knew that we already had plans for other accommodations.

Anticipation built as we headed up the steps to the Lochsa station. Most of the site was a museum. We walked into the office and met Gail, a mature woman that worked as an interpreter. Unbelievably, there was no phone at the station, and Gail told us that the nearest phone was forty miles east at the Powell Ranger Station or twenty miles west in Lowell. My hopes of finally talking to my family were dashed, and we walked out feeling quite disappointed. The only good part of all of this was that we were at our meeting point for Kris, and there was a campground one mile east up the road.

As we walked down the steps to the parking lot, a retired couple from Florida named Ellis and Marie Ware pulled in with their RV bus. We asked if they had a car phone, knowing that there probably wasn't an available service cell, even if they did. They said they did not but would be willing to make a call for me when they got to Lowell. I wrote a message for the Wares to give to Kris, hoping it would not alarm her. It simply said that we were out early, but OK, and that she could pick us up earlier on Wednesday if it was convenient. If not, Thursday would still be fine. While I was talking to the Florida couple, Todd and Susie were playing with two puppies that were riding with a trucker from Montana. They were both Labrador retrievers, one black and one yellow, each about six months old. Before Marie and Ellis drove off, they asked all three of us if we would like a Coke. Checking with each other to see if we heard correctly, we jumped at the chance and politely accepted their offer – not believing that we would be drinking anything as extravagant as Coca Cola today after four days of little water or water that tasted like iodine due to our water purification system. Pulling out a storage compartment from the side of their deluxe RV, Ellis handed us each an ice cold can of Coke. We thanked them again, said good-bye and returned to the steps leading up to the ranger station to savor our civilized beverage. I wondered how much Lewis and Clark missed the little comforts of home when they were on their journey.

Well, after our Cokes were finished, we were in a much better and much sillier mood. We hiked our packs back to the Wilderness Gateway campsites and found a scenic spot by the river. The sites cost six dollars per night, but all we had was two dollars in cash and a $100 travelers check. This posed a problem for us because the correct and exact dollar amount had to be placed in an envelope and deposited in a locked metal box via a letter slot. We decided to camp and talk the ranger into letting us pay on Wednesday when the RV and our cash arrived.

We built a campfire, as we had the night before, and went to sleep at 10:30 under a three-quarter moon.

TUESDAY, JULY 19, 1994

This was quite a varied day for me. In the morning, we were entertained by the multitude of ground squirrels that live in the campground. Apparently they have been fed by other visitors, so they are quite brave and come very close to you. If you are not careful, they will go through your packs in search of food.

Bolstered by yesterday's experience, I decided after breakfast that I would try to hitch a ride into Lowell, Idaho, which is twenty-four miles west, in order to call home and make sure Kris got the message from the Wares and was not worried. I started talking to some people around our campsite, hinting for a ride, and had an interesting conversation with two people, a retired couple named Boyd and Nida Harrison from Lewiston, who were camped in their trailer across the road. They had been camping in this campground for years, and I told them why we were here and all about the difficulties we had with water and trail markers. They told an interesting story about a man and woman that hiked out of the Wilderness Gateway campground, where we were, four years ago. They were staying five sites down from us and had decided to hike up on the ridge. What they did not expect was for their day to become a deadly lesson in following basic hiking guidelines.

It seems that they were following a trail and decided to abandon it, perhaps for water. One thing led to another, and they became disoriented and lost. They finally found a stream and decided to follow the streambed, hoping it would lead down to the Lochsa River and Route 12. Apparently it was a very grueling hike, so much so that, despite words of encouragement from the man, the woman reached a point of total exhaustion and collapsed beside a tree. Four days after they had left, the man, most certainly dehydrated and totally exhausted, was spotted by campers crossing the Lochsa River and returning to camp alone. When he was met by others, he informed them that his companion was dead. The first rescue helicopter that was called refused to search for individuals if they were confirmed dead, so a second rescue helicopter was summoned from Granger. When they reached the body, they found that rigor mortis had "frozen" the woman's body in a sitting position, and they were unable to secure her body to the stretcher. They wondered how they would extricate her from the ridgeside location. After many long, sad hours at the Wilderness Gateway Campground, campers were given a shocking and macabre sight as a helicopter was finally spotted returning down the river valley, intending to land across the river from the campground where emergency vehicles were parked. Dangling from a rescue rope underneath the helicopter was the woman's body supported by a harness, still in the sitting position in which she died. There was not a dry eye in the campground, but there was a very hard lesson learned in the precautions that should be taken and followed when hiking in the wilderness.

This story was amazing to hear from people that had witnessed it, and, on a side note, proved even more timely because there are currently four people presumed lost in this forest. Two search helicopters flew over this morning. The lost people are two days late returning from their hike, and the only possible lead was from the pilot of a small plane that spotted four individuals hiking by a lake up in the thick forest.

After the story was finished, Boyd told me that he was going fishing and could give me a ride to the Lochsa Historical Ranger Station. I accepted, thinking it was a start and would at least get me out to Route 12. During our drive, I explained again how I was a teacher, what we were doing and why I needed to call my family. Boyd told me how he used to hunt up on and around the Lolo Trail area when he was fourteen to nineteen years old. During one of the trips, he remembered spotting a very old and large set of wheels down in a ravine. He thought nothing of it at the time, but years later he spoke to someone who was searching for General Howard's lost cannon that supposedly had rolled off the trail as it was being transported and never recovered. Howard Camp, one of our campsites on the Lolo Trail was named after General Howard. Boyd told him about his sighting and was eager to go back and locate it; however, it was never found. It might have been destroyed or covered by debris. Given the way snow changes the terrain in northern Idaho and the length of time between Boyd's visits, it is quite possible that the search was in the wrong location. The possibility exists that General Howard's cannon, or the remains of it, is still waiting to be discovered by a sharp-eyed backpacker or hunter somewhere along the Lolo Trail in Idaho.

After I was dropped off at the ranger station, I decided to go up and ask Gail if she knew of anyone that was going west to Lowell. She said that she did not know of someone but would be willing to spread the word to visitors that came in and suggested that I wait at the bottom of the steps. Seeing that it was already 10:00 A.M., I decided to try my luck on the road.

Not much traffic was on Route 12 at this time of day, so I was forced to wait for awhile in between cars that were traveling west. During this time, I heard Todd calling to me from somewhere up in the forest on the opposite side of the river across the road. Try as I might, I could not locate him, so I yelled hello and waved blindly toward the area where his shouts were coming from.

Luckily, after about twenty minutes, a blue Honda Accord with Montana plates and driven by a middle aged man in a white shirt and blue tie pulled over. He introduced himself as Craig, and I introduced myself and told him where I was wanting to go. He said that he was on his way to Lewiston. Perfect! Craig's car was air conditioned, which felt wonderful after standing in the sun. I told Craig about the trip I was on, and he seemed extremely interested. After a few minutes he said that he thought I looked familiar. He had heard about our trip and said he was from Great Falls. I told him that it was possible that he had read about it in the paper, since many press releases were sent out to the towns through which we would be passing on our itinerary. Craig seemed to think that someone had told him the story, perhaps his secretary, but he was not sure who it could have been. Then he thought that it might have been a TV news program, and I remembered the spontaneous interview that we had done on the sidewalks of Great Falls. Things started to fall into place from then on. Craig recalled information that he could not have known otherwise such as our six hour, ten mile day's ordeal with the wind north of Fort Peck. He also said that a blond haired man on the sports section of the ABC news program had run the story. Yes, that was it! I couldn't believe the odds of being picked up by someone that knew who I was and had heard about our trip. The remainder of the ride was spent educating Craig about the Lewis and Clark expedition. He asked many questions and was extremely interested in learning more about it. As I sat in the car, my thoughts turned to whether this occurrence was due to luck, guardian angels and/or additional intervention from our unseen partner and guide.

We finally arrived in Lowell. I thanked Craig for the ride and got out of his car feeling very fortunate for such a good experience. Except for Erin's ride yesterday, I have never hitchhiked, nor wanted to, before now, and I found myself rating the cars that approached in relation to the types of people that might be driving them. I felt bad for judging people by the vehicles they drove but considered it my only means of screening the people in this necessary, yet risky, activity. I had no other option for getting to a phone. At least I was half way through my hitching experience. I was in Lowell and had only to call home and make it back to the campground.

As Craig drove away, I was struck by the size of Lowell: three buildings, that I could see, on the northern side of Route 12. One was a motel, the second was a diner/restaurant and the third was a combination souvenir/service station/store. My eye was then drawn to a sign which read "Welcome to Lowell. Population 24 23." Wow! Talk about your small towns. This had to be one of the smallest I had seen and looked like an interesting stop.

I headed for the restaurant called the Wilderness Inn. The AT&T sticker on the door satisfied my question about the telephone availability. Sure enough, just inside the door was a phone, and I wasted no time dialing home. The call went through, and I was hoping that Kris would be home since it was 2:30 P.M. in New Jersey. She answered, we agreed where to pick-up, and I spoke to Melina, who seemed excited to leave and wanted to know if I had any funny stories to tell.

After hanging up the phone at 11:45 A.M. my eye was drawn to the counter and the menu. I asked if they could cash a traveler's check, which they could, and I ordered a hamburger, fries and a piece of coconut custard pie. They served some of the largest portions that I have ever seen, and it tasted like heaven after four days of freeze dried camping food. A television was turned on above the counter, and I noted that the television station was broadcasting from Denver, Colorado. One of the stories was about today being the 25th anniversary of the first moon walk, and I was reminded of Dayton Duncan's comparison of the Lewis and Clark expedition to the space program; each was exploring the current frontier for our country. After finishing my pie, I thought it would be nice to surprise

Susie and Todd with some "real" food. I ordered two cheeseburgers and two pieces of apple pie "to go," waited for my order, paid at the counter and walked to the other side of Route 12 to try my luck at getting a ride back to the campground.

I don't think that more than half a dozen cars went by before a blue Toyota 4x4 truck pulled over with a mountain bike attached to the roof. A young guy in sunglasses said that he was pulling in to get a sandwich at the Wilderness Inn but was willing to give me a ride if I wanted to wait. In the meantime, I was free to try my luck on the road. As he pulled into the parking lot, I decided not to push my luck any further and walked back to wait for my ride by the truck. I felt I was again being cared for and watched over by someone or something and could sense that taking this ride was the right thing for me to do.

A few minutes later the driver came out, introduced himself as Mike, and we pulled out heading east. Mike said that he was a recent college graduate working for the Nez Perce National Forest. He is an avid cyclist, hiker and kayaker, and we hit it off very well. His degree is in botany, and I mentioned that my father used to be a botany professor at Fairleigh Dickinson University in Madison, NJ. Mike was also extremely interested in the Quest West trip. During our discussions, I asked Mike what he was doing over the summer, and he said that he was working with someone who had a Ph.D. in botany. They formed a team along with nineteen others to ground truth the satellite pictures of foliage in the forest. Basically they went out into the forest and recorded the types of trees and shrubs that were in different quadrants of the forest photos. In this way scientists could learn to correlate different colors on the satellite photos with specific tree species. Very interesting! We discussed fire policy and how the National Parks were slowly starting to see the value of fires in the natural progression of the forest and other environments. Mike was a free spirit who had experience riding 1,200-mile bike tours and hitchhiking throughout Canada and the U.S. He said he almost always picked up people that wanted a ride because of his own experiences. Mike insisted on driving me into the camp loop road, and, amidst final comments about fire policies and benefits, I again appreciated my good fortune in having had two excellent drivers and in making it back with lunch for Todd and Susie by 12:45 P.M.

Todd and Susie were on a walk and returned to our campsite at about 1:20 ready for lunch but expecting to have PB&J on pita bread. They were interested in finding out what had happened to me, but they were even more surprised when I pulled out the bags of cheeseburgers and pie after tantalizing them with the story of my lunch.

The river here is really beautiful, and I spent most of the afternoon exploring amidst the water and rocks while my satisfied companions napped under the tent's rain sheet. Later on, while returning from a water refill, Nida Harrison called me into their campsite and asked me if I liked fish. When I said I did, Boyd came out of his RV with two frozen cutthroat trout that he had caught this morning on the Lochsa River. He said that he had plenty, and we were welcome to them if we wanted. This seemed too good to be true, but I gratefully accepted the trout and returned to camp with looks of amazement on Todd's and Susie's faces. Mine showed the same amazed expression, I'm sure. We were being provided with the things we needed. No longer did I feel these events to be luck.

One of our campground hosts has given us a hard time about not having money to pay for the campsite despite explanations about how this was an unforeseen twist in our plans and that the RV, which would be here on Wednesday or Thursday, would have the correct amount of money. We would definitely pay at that point. All the money we now had consisted of large bills and two $1.00 bills. The site cost $6.00 per night, and we didn't have the exact amount. While in Lowell, I was able to cash the traveler's check but was so intent on talking to my family and getting lunch that correct change for the campground completely slipped my mind. Anyway, as I went to get water with Todd after dinner, we passed the hosts, a man and a woman. The woman had earlier mentioned the rangers OK to our situation, but I guess the gentleman felt like he had to say something. He reminded us that we were against regulations because we should have paid one half hour after choosing our site. He also indicated that he did not think we intended to pay. This upset me since he was now attacking our character; however, we told him that we were honest people, and the campground would get their money. I even offered to pay him with a $20.00 bill if he could give us change. His response was that the money had to be put in the box. I left, thinking of how to respond to the situation. As far as I was concerned, if the ranger had given the OK, these confrontations were not necessary, yet our host was making me uncomfortable. I decided to go to other campsites to try and find change for my $20.00 bill. This would allow us to register and put this situation behind us. No one to whom I spoke could help, but, once again, on my return trip to our site, Nida called me over to their campsite where she was playing Scrabble with Boyd. They offered to help me out with correct change, and I was able to exchange my $20.00 bill for three "fives" and five "ones" . . . another unrequested provision. I knew that I could now pay the correct amount and did so promptly in order to silence our "hosts."

On the way back to our campsite, I asked the Harrison's their recommendations on cooking trout. Nida asked me if we had a pan, to which I had to admit we did not. As soon as I admitted this, Boyd came out of his RV with a large, black, cast iron skillet and said that it would do the trick. Accepting graciously, I was then asked if we had bread crumbs. Before I could answer completely, Boyd invited me into their RV for "fixings." He gave me a small baggie full of bread crumbs and a container of vegetable oil to put in the pan for cooking. I left feeling extremely grateful and a little embarrassed of how much Nida and Boyd had done for us. They have both been a huge help to us over the past two days. Todd and I are looking forward to giving them Quest West T-shirts when Kris and Melina arrive with our support vehicle. We can't wait for trout tomorrow morning! It will be a fantastic beginning to the day when I will finally be reunited with my family. I'm so excited!

Dinner tonight was large.

We basically ate everything that was left except for tomorrow's breakfast and lunch materials for tomorrow. Excellent! Our day ended as it had for the past few days – with a campfire before bed. I have good feelings and much anticipation for the day ahead.

MERIWETHER LEWIS – THURSDAY JUNE 13TH 1805.

My fare is really sumptuous this evening; buffaloe's humps, tongues and marrowbones, fine trout parched meal pepper and salt, and a good appetite; the last is not considered the least of the luxuries.

WEDNESDAY, JULY 20, 1994

The big day finally had arrived. I awoke early and took my daily bath and solo down by the river. Breakfast was great. While I was at the river, Todd had gotten up and filleted the trout that Boyd and Nida had given us. We cooked it in the pan that they loaned to us and fried the trout in the bread crumbs and oil. It was exquisite! We also took this opportunity to eat any remaining food that we had with us. It was a feast.

After breakfast we cleaned up camp and hiked up the river trail to sit and swim at a spot that had a beach. The Lochsa River between our camp and Lowell is dotted with several, small sand beaches at places where the river has deposited material. Todd and Susie had a refreshing swim, and I took photos, one of which was of a little green snake that was darting in and out of the rocks in the water along the shore.

I walked back to our campsite at 1:30 and returned the pan, oil and bread crumbs to Nida and Boyd. They told me a story about how they knew John Fogerty of Credence Clearwater Revival fame. He lives in Oregon. The Harrisons live in Lewiston, and their son used to play with CCR in the very early days before the band began recording.

I took a photograph of the Harrisons, and we exchanged addresses.

Then the time came to wait for Kris and Melina. It seemed like forever to me, and I did a great deal of pacing, but they arrived at 4:00 P.M. It was one of the best feelings that I've ever had. I can't remember hugs ever feeling so good. Melina didn't want to let go of me. It seems their flight was delayed by one hour. Thankfully, Melina was able to sleep on the drive from Missoula to our campground. We walked across the camp road, so that Melina and Kris could meet the Harrisons, and we gave Boyd and Nida each a Quest West T-shirt. They loved the shirts and wanted to take our photograph as well.

After saying good-bye to the Harrisons, we drove our RV to Grangeville, Idaho where we checked in to an RV park and went out for a large reunion dinner, which was also much anticipated. It was comforting to know that we were all finally together. We'll be off to Riggins, Idaho tomorrow where our friends from New Jersey had offered us an evening in their lodge and a rafting trip down the Salmon River with Exodus, their river touring company.

dinner at the Wilderness Gateway Campground

Nida (L) and Boyd (R) Harrison

Part 5

Idaho and Eastern Washington

roadside wildflowers

Thursday, July 21, 1994

We woke up this morning at the RV campground and went to breakfast at Copper Hood Pizza. Although I have been known to eat pizza in the morning, this meal was the traditional eggs, pancakes and the like, and it was very good. Feeling very full, we drove to Riggins but not before doing some shopping in Grangeville. The drive into Riggins was all downhill, and I am worried about the Rig making it back up such a steep, consistent hill. I have noticed that our current environment is much different from that around the Lochsa River. This area down by Riggins is much more stark and no longer supports a vast amount of trees.

We arrived in Riggins, stopped in Exodus for directions to the Bradbury family's lodge and proceeded to our destination along a winding, narrow road. Several times I had to pull over to let logging trucks go past us because the road is basically one lane in width with steep embankments and/or dropoffs on either side. One bank led up the mountainside, and the other led down to the river. We have been told that several accidents have occurred on the road, with some resulting in the loss of life.

When we got to our destination, we encountered a narrow, suspension bridge, which was the only means of crossing the Salmon River to the lodge. We debated about crossing with the Rig, finally deciding to give it a try. Todd directed, as I nervously steered our way onto the bridge. Well, the Rig proved to be too large to make it completely under the bridge supports, and, for a moment, we feared that we were going to be stuck on the bridge. I felt a bit like the Grinch squeezing down a chimney. Eventually, the Rig made it out, and we had to park on the side of the road in a pull-off lot and carry what we could across the bridge. Janice Bradbury greeted us and offered us a golf cart to shuttle the rest of our bags over to the lodge from the Rig.

The lodge was an oasis – beautiful trees surrounded by a lush and level lawn, which was nothing like the surrounding, brown, rugged hillsides. The building itself was made of logs, and there was a pool which was fed with water from hot springs. The water was a consistent 96 degrees. During earlier times, Native Americans would come to this place to bathe in the hot water and take advantage of the medicinal qualities that were believed to be present in the mud surrounding the springs.

All of us loved the place. Melina played with two kittens that were on our deck. Janice is an excellent host! It wasn't long before we were introduced to Bert, the chef. She is very skilled and serves excellent food as evidenced by the swordfish that was served for dinner. Our mouths were watering long before sitting down to the table from the delicious aromas wafting out from the kitchen, and now we are eagerly looking forward to breakfast! We have been so focused on food during this trip, primarily as a source of energy, and now it was a welcome luxury to enjoy its fine preparation, aesthetic appeal and abundance.

We all went for a hot spring dip in the pool after dinner, complete with our plush, white, terrycloth robes, which were laid out for each of us in our rooms. The hot tub temperature was 106°! Needless to say, we are all relaxed, happy to be together and literally soaking up these hedonistic pleasures.

MERIWETHER LEWIS – THURSDAY MAY 9TH 1805.

Capt. C. killed two bucks and 2 buffaloe, I also killed one buffaloe which proved to be the best meat, it was in tolerable order; we saved the best of the meat, and from the cow I killed we saved the necessary materials for making what our wrighthand cook Charbono calls the boudin (poudingue) blanc, and immediately set him about preparing them for supper; this white pudding we all esteem one of the greatest delacies of the forrest, it may not be amiss therefore to give it a place. About 6 feet of the lower extremity of the large gut of the Buffaloe is the first mosel that the cook makes love to, this he holds fast at one end with the right hand, while with the forefinger and thumb of the left he gently compresses it, and discharges what he says is not good to eat, but of which in the s[e]quel we get a moderate portion; the mustle lying underneath the shoulder blade next to the back, and fillets are next saught, these are needed up very fine with a good portion of kidney suit; to this composition is then added a just proportion of pepper and salt and a small quantity of flour; thus far advanced, our skilfull operator C____o seizes his recepticle, which has never once touched the water, for that would entirely distroy the regular order of the whole procedure; you will not forget that the side you now see is that covered with a good coat of fat provided the animal be in good order; the operator sceizes the recepticle I say, and tying it fast at one end turns it inward and begins now with repeated evolutions of the hand and arm, and a brisk motion of the finger and thumb to put in what he says is bon pour manger;   thus by stuffing and compressing he soon distends the recepticle to the utmost limmits of it's power of expansion, and in the course of it's longtudinal progress it drives from the other end of the recepticle a much larger portion of the [blank space in MS.] than was prevously discharged by the finger and thumb of the left hand in a former part of the operation; thus when the sides of the recepticle are skilfully exchanged the outer for the inner, and all is compleatly filled with something good to eat, it is tyed at the other end, but not any cut off, for that would make the pattern too scant;   it is then baptised in the missouri with two dips and a flirt, and bobbed into the kettle; from whence, after it be well boiled it is taken and fryed with bears oil untill it becomes brown, when it is ready to esswage the pangs of a keen appetite or such as travelers in the wilderness are seldom at a loss for.

FRIDAY, JULY 22, 1994

Breakfast consisted of puffed apple pancake and all the trimmings. Bert had outdone herself again! We were reluctant to leave our comfortable surroundings, but all of us were looking forward to the rafting trip. Lewis and Clark did not travel down the rough watered Salmon River on the advise of the Shoshoni Indians. Even the Shoshoni had not navigated down what is still called "The River of No Return." This portion of the trip was pure fun for us and a well-timed break.

It was arranged for us to meet Brian, our guide, on the river bank when our trip began at 10:30 A.M. The Salmon River, as Brian described, changed daily and seasonally, and it was one of the few remaining rivers that were still "free" and not controlled by dams. Today the water was low. The rapids were fun, but the day was long and hot. Lunch was provided by Exodus, the rafting company, and it accompanied us on the raft. We ate on a sand beach where we also took the opportunity to do some exploring and swimming. Melina loved the water. Later on, we took turns jumping over the side of the raft to float in the river current. Swimming with Melina was great fun, and floating in the river current is a wonderful, almost weightless feeling.

Our trip on the river ended at 7:30 P.M. For such a long day on the river – 9 hours – Melina was excellent, but we were all tired and a bit sunburned despite the use of sunscreen.

Dinner was at Somerville's Diner in Riggins. It was decided, because it was 9:00 P.M. when we finished eating, that we would stay in the Bruce Motel in Riggins. It cost $26.00 per night with a free RV hook up. Todd and Susie are spending the night in the RV. Kris, Melina and I are going to sleep in the motel room. It is a very hot evening!

SATURDAY, JULY 23, 1994

Melina, Kris and I began our day at 7:00 A.M. with a twelve-year-old boy peeping into our window. Upon his return with his mother, I asked, rather abruptly after throwing open the curtains, if I could help them. The mother responded by saying they didn't know if anyone was in the room.

We pulled out of the Bruce Motel at about 8:30 A.M. Mountain Time, and it quickly changed to 7:30 A.M. as we passed over the Riggins Bridge and into Pacific Time once again. The Rig had a hard time making it up White Bird Hill which is really a small mountain. Below us on the plains was an area famous for Indian battles. We retraced our journey from Thursday back to Kooskia and up to Kamiah. Our final destination was the Lewis and Clark RV Park just 1.3 miles south of Kamiah.

Our day was rather uneventful, but we spent the time watching frogs in the pond, gathering peacock feathers from the birds kept in the park, picking string beans in the RV park community garden, swimming in the pool and cleaning our bikes. It was very hot . . . 100 degrees or so. We were pleasantly surprised to notice the RV of Ellis and Marie Ware, the couple from Florida that gave us Cokes at the Lochsa Historical Ranger Station and made a phone call to Kris for us. Their site was across the campground, but I assume they went to town for the evening because their car was not in tow, and no one was inside when I knocked.

We have noticed that the people traveling in recreational vehicles and trailers often resemble a mobile community. Many of them know each other, and, whether planned or

Gordon and Melina floating in the Salmon River

not, they often cross paths at different locations. In many ways these RV travelers are like extended family to one and other, and I can't help making the comparison to the hard core Grateful Dead supporters, A.K.A. Deadheads, that follow the band from concert to concert. The mobile lifestyle and the common interests become familiar and rewarding bonding agents for them all.

After a dinner of pasta, Todd noticed that the grey water in the RV had backed up into the tub and soaked a good deal of our riding gear that was stored in there. This led to a major hosing off and clean up. Our day ended with another dip in the pool. I have replotted our daily destinations, so Kris, Melina and Susie can be in a RV park every night. It helps, with so many people, to have a place to shower and do the laundry. It should also make the eastern Washington desert crossing easier on us all. Tomorrow we will be back on our bikes, and I'm looking forward to it. We hope to be out of here and on the road by 8:00 A.M. at the latest. We'll see what happens. Hopefully the clouds that rolled in late this afternoon will linger to provide for a cooler day tomorrow than we had today.

SUNDAY, JULY 24, 1994

Today was Susie's birthday. Todd planned to take her out to eat as soon as we got to Lewiston, Idaho. We've got a fifty-six mile ride today to Nez Perce Historical Park in Lewiston. We'll see how it goes.

We started our ride at 8:07 A.M. as we pulled away from the Lewis and Clark RV Park. The ride was beautiful and downhill all the way. We also did not have to buck headwinds. As a result, we made excellent time. Along the way, we passed a site where Lewis and Clark descended to the Clearwater River. From here they went sixteen miles up to get canoes.

Todd and I stopped in a town called Orafino where we found they were having a 1950s celebration. Events included a parade on Saturday, and today's activities included a 1950s car and truck show on the fairgrounds where there must have been thirty to forty vehicles. This provided a great chance to stop, walk for a while and get something to drink. I thought I had a broken spoke as we rode into town, but it proved to be only a rubbing sound that was eliminated by truing up the rear wheel. As we rode down the main street, one could hear early rock and roll music playing. They were piping it through the streets, but the streets were deserted – no one on the streets, just the '50s music. It was kind of cool, yet a bit eerie. It reminded me of a setting in a Ray Bradbury novel. I guess everyone was at the celebration at Orofino City Park. Riding out of Orofino, Todd and I noticed that some of these roads have a painted message on them that says, "Don't be a Gooberish." We don't know what this means, but we would like to find out.

Once we were back on the road, it didn't take long to get to Lewiston. The Rig passed and then pulled over for us about three miles before our turnoff for the Nez Perce National Historical Park. Impeccable timing! We put our bikes on the Rig and headed down to the park which was a couple miles south on Route 95. Melina enjoyed seeing the Native American exhibits. She asked me why there weren't any more Indians. I explained that there were, but that their dress and customs had changed. (Sometimes it's hard to be proud of this country's history.)

It was now extremely hot, although we didn't know at the time how hot it actually was. Todd and I decided to push onward and ride the remaining ten or twelve miles to the camp-site. It ended up being the worst part of the ride, as Route 12, our original road, merged with Route 95, and the road became a divided highway with a great deal of trucks and traffic. The heat, which radiated off of the highway, and the hot wind that hit our faces made it feel like we had hot hair dryers blowing on us. The heat robs us of energy and water and has made me dizzy on occasion. There was little shelter from it. We also encountered the stench in the air from a paper company, which was very unpleasant to breath while riding, and we couldn't escape it – quite a change from 190 years ago! Lewiston is considerably developed and urban. However, what we will remember about the city is the heat. Upon riding through town, we were surprised to see the thermometers on two banks read 114°!

We finally got to our site at Hell's Gate State Park. Given the current temperature the name seemed quite appropriate. It was a very nice location, but it was just too hot, and the air conditioning in the Rig was not working. After watching a fighter jet from a nearby air show do maneuvers and tricks overhead, we decided to find relief in a motel in town. We ended up staying in the Tapadera Inn. Melina went swimming with Kris while I napped. Later, Kris, Melina and I went out to eat at a place called Panhandler Pies while Todd and Susie explored around town. We had wonderful food for dinner, and there were twenty-eight different kinds of very good pies. Their fresh Strawberry, Mounds of Joy, and Razzleberry pies were all sampled, as we each tried a different kind. I confess that I went back for the Razzleberry, a combination of raspberry, blueberry and boysenberry, at 9:00 P.M. Pie became somewhat of a tradition for Todd and me to eat on the trip. It seemed to be a much more popular dessert out west, and it provided quick energy for us on the road.

We watched a wicked lightning storm roll through the area after dark. It was quite a light show! Before we ride tomorrow, Todd and I have to make some phone calls, and we need to get the Rig's steps and air conditioning fixed so they work correctly. It would be nice to have the air conditioning working for Susie, Kris and Melina, especially in the Washington desert where temperatures are supposed to be hovering between 108° and 112° for the next few days.

MERIWETHER LEWIS – FRIDAY JULY 19TH 1805
>   . . . *we are almost suffocated in this confined valley with heat.*

WILLIAM CLARK – OCTOBER 6TH SATURDAY (SUNDAY) 1805
>   . . . *all the Canoes finished this evening ready to be put into the water. . . .*
>   . . . *The river below this forks is Called Kos-kos-kee   it is Clear rapid with Shoals or Swift places*
>   *The open Countrey Commences a fiew miles below this on each side of the river, . . .*

Monday, July 25, 1994

After breakfast in Panhandler Pies Restaurant, we made a quick trip to see if someone could recharge the freon in the air conditioner and the refrigerator. Neither one is doing the job. Our ride, therefore, was late to begin, and we set off at 11:21 A.M. At 11:30 A.M. we crossed the Snake River and entered Washington. The Rig passed us fifteen miles into our trip, and at that point we all decided to meet in Pomeroy for lunch, which we did.

The second half of our day was spent fighting headwinds, hills (one that was three miles long), and the incredible, building heat in the Washington desert. My legs refused to work at one point, and I was forced to stop, stretch and rest for a bit.

Our campsite in Lewis and Clark Trail State Park was beautiful, surrounded by tall pines and nicely set up when we arrived at 6:45 P.M. Kris, Melina and Susie did a spectacular job getting things ready. We had chicken for dinner, but Todd narrowly missed being burned when the escaping propane from the grill blew up in his face upon lighting it. The experience was quite unsettling! We put in 74.6 miles today, and, given the heat and the hills, it was our toughest ride to date. Melina and I plan to sleep in the tent. Thunderstorms are a possibility tonight.

TUESDAY, JULY 26, 1994

An intense but local thunderstorm blew through our campsite and park last night. At one point I thought that we might need to sleep in the Rig for safety purposes. One clap of thunder sounded directly over our tent, which finally woke Melina. Since it turned out to be the last of the thunder, we settled down again for the rest of the night.

Morning brought telephone calls to Adrianne Go at the *Tri Cities Herald* and other reporters, along with additional calls to contacts offering to put us up for a night. We had planned to stay with an alum of FHCDS that lives in Portland, but it seems he will be on vacation during the time we will be going through the city. This means alternative plans for lodging will have to be made for the Portland area.

Our ride began late at 10:00 A.M., but we were lucky to pass through a number of towns on our way to the Arrowhead Campground & RV Park in Pasco. The graphic patterns that we have noticed in the surrounding fields are very striking.

They are due to strip farming. Different and distinct areas of crops of varying colors have been planted on the surrounding hillsides and create striped or patchwork patterns that are quite beautiful.

It actually rained a little bit before we got to Prescott, Washington, which turned out to be a great little town with a pool, tennis courts and a general store. God! I just had Twinkies that I bought in the general store for a snack! Shhh! Don't tell anybody! Apple strudel and apple juice was also on the snack menu.

Another interesting place that we happened upon was Frank Brojke (pronounced Brochee) Farm & Orchards. Todd and I had ridden through Eureka searching for a place to eat lunch. There wasn't any, but we did speak to a wheat farmer that was familiar with the east coast. His wife went to NYU. He told us we could find a place to eat in the orchard community. It turns out that orchards encompass three thousand acres of apple trees and employs a significant number of workers, largely Mexican in heritage. To accommodate them, a community was created that includes quality housing, a church, a school, a day care facility and a convenience/grocery/deli store called Jo-Jo's Market. We found the community and had a very good lunch of fried chicken.

During our last few miles of the day, we were passed by a white Subaru. A man leaned out of the window and asked if we were Gordon and Todd. We stopped and learned that they were from KVEW-TV, the ABC Channel 42 in Kennewick, WA. They did an interview

graphic patterns due to strip farming

and shot some footage of us riding on Route 124. It was an exciting way to end the ride, and they told us we could watch the piece between 5:30 and 6:00 that afternoon.

When we met the Rig at the junction of 124 and 12, we cooled off, went for a swim in the Snake River at a local park and headed for our campground. It seems that Priscilla Miller had contacted KVEW, and calls had been made through the Rig's phone, so Susie, Kris and Melina knew about the interview we had. However, they told us that Katie Aldrich from KEPR, Channel 19 from Yakima, WA, wanted to do a more in-depth story tomorrow morning. Her station serves the Tri-City area as well. When we arrived at Arrowhead Campground, Todd called Katie and set up an interview and filming at the park where we ended our ride today. We are scheduled to meet her at 9:00 A.M. tomorrow.

Dinner tonight was out at the Country Gentleman Restaurant in Pasco. We are about to enter a more scenic area of Washington, and we are looking forward to the visual difference and temperature change. Washington is called the pine tree state, but you wouldn't know it by the way we entered. The evergreens are in the more moderate, western region of the state. Today it was 99° . . . better, but still hot.

WILLIAM CLARK – OCTOBER 16TH WEDNESDAY 1805

. . . *Set out and proceeded on Seven miles to the junction of this river [the Snake] and the Columbia which joins from the N.W. In every direction from the junction of those rivers the countrey is one continued plain low and rises from the water gradually, except a range of high Countrey which runs from S.W. & N.E. and is on the opposit Side about 2 miles distant from the Collumbia and keeping its derection S.W. untill it joins a S.W. range of mountains.*

WEDNESDAY, JULY 27, 1994

Our ride today took us from Pasco to Crow Butte State Park near Paterson. Katie Aldrich interviewed us at 9:00 A.M. in Hood Park and shot a good deal of videotape of Todd and me riding on the road. She was very interested in our adventure and will be mailing a tape home for us to keep.

We started today's ride at 10:23 A.M. and rode along the Columbia River for a good deal of the way.

We passed a paper mill that had the most awful odor coming from it. In the processing I believe that chemicals are added to the paper, but, for whatever reason, the process smells terrible. We just couldn't wait to get out of the wind pattern. So, for the time being we were lookin' at the Columbia River that's flowing south on our right. The river soon changed direction and flowed west, and we dipped down south into Oregon for a bit and then caught up with the Columbia again when we crossed the Route 82/395 bridge.

There was a stop for pictures along Route 730 going towards Hermiston. As soon as we got into the river gorge, we saw a very long freight train on the Washington side of the

route along the Columbia River

Columbia River. Todd counted ninety-four cars. Terns and Pelicans were diving into the water, and we found that we had a headwind from that point onward, but we felt good about the ride.

When we got to Hermiston, we met Todd Chamberlain from the Hermiston Herald. He was basically writing a story from the press release but wanted a photo to go with it. We also had lunch in the Crooked Tree Bakery and Cafe. I treated myself to an avocado deluxe sandwich and a vast amount to drink. Todd had a Toll House Pie and a French Dip sandwich. It was really good, and they make their own bread and pies. After lunch in Hermiston, we rode to the campsite since it was just a little ways west of the Interstate 82 bridge.

Crow Butte State Park was like an oasis in the desert, and we all had fun swimming in the Columbia River. We plan to get an early start tomorrow to avoid some of the heat.

SERGEANT JOHN ORDWAY – FRIDAY 18TH OCT. 1805

a clear pleasant morning. . . . we proceeded on down the great Columbia River which is now verry wide about 3/4 of a mile in General   the country in general Smooth plains for about 10 miles down then the barron hills make close to the River on each Side. . . .

THURSDAY, JULY 28, 1994

Today was a fifty-four mile ride from Crow Butte State Park to Maryhill State Park. It was cool in the morning, and it was nice to get an early start. We had another clear and sunny day, but this meant that the heat would soon return, so, again, I'm glad we got off to an early start. Todd and I left at 7:30 A.M., only to find two miles out that I did not have my water bottles with me. After a brief trip back to the Rig, we headed west on Route 14. There was nothing on the road except trucks, but they were not as concentrated as they were in the afternoon.

I am growing tired of the monotone, desert landscape, but I am trying hard to appreciate it for its unique characteristics. Todd and I are also weary of fighting constant headwinds, and my hands are beginning to ache. It's an uncomfortable sensation that spreads up my arms and into my shoulders due to my hands becoming numb when riding. The pressure from the handlebars must push on a nerve, and I cannot find a hand position to relieve it.

Both of us welcomed the opportunity to stop for a snack in Roosevelt. I believe the name of this little restaurant was the Wood Gulch Cafe. Todd and I left our bikes on the front, plywood porch, and ordered pancakes with honey and hash browns. As we were sitting there, pies came out of the oven, so, of course, we had to order pie and ended up with a couple of hot slices of blueberry pie a la mode. Good fuel for what lay ahead.

At 10:19 A.M., we left the cafe and were back on Route 14 with thirty-two miles still to go. We spotted Mount Hood, capped in snow, when we were one half mile west of Roosevelt.

This was a definite milestone for us. This was also the view that let Lewis and Clark know they were back on the map, as Mount Hood was noted by Captain Grey when he sailed his ship partially up the Columbia in 1792.

our first sighting of Mount Hood

During our sixty-four mile ride, the only other break came when the Rig passed us about six miles out of Roosevelt and everyone pulled off the road for a rest. Our ride was hard. My back started to cramp up, and I had to dismount a couple of times to stretch out. Our water was so hot that it ceased to be refreshing at all. To make matters worse, we hit a hill during the last six miles of our ride that climbed steeply for two miles and left me with very little energy. All of the frustration and exhaustion got the better of me when we reached our camp, and I literally threw my bike to the ground. There was nothing I wanted more at that moment than rest.

After we got to the campsite at Maryhill State Park, we showered and then drove to the Maryhill Art Museum. It is situated about two miles west of the intersection of Routes 14 and 97 along the Washington side of the Columbia River. As we found, this museum has an extensive collection of Rodin sculptures, chess sets from around the world, American paintings and Native American artifacts. This museum is amazing, especially considering where it is located. It's removed from anything I would consider to be a populated area. Before we left, we took in the view from the museum, which looked across the river and over our campsite area. The hills on the opposite side of the Columbia River were charred and still smoldering from a wildfire that burned the night before we arrived. It seems that it began up near a chicken farm and spread down toward the river.

From the museum, we all went to dinner and had ice cream back at the park. The headwind has taken a considerable toll on our bodies, so Todd and I decided to take a day off from riding tomorrow and explore some of the local sites instead.

PRIVATE JOSEPH WHITEHOUSE – SUNDAY 3RD NOV. 1805.
a foggy morning. . . . we Saw a high round mountain on the Lard. Side which we expect is the Same we Saw abo. the great falls and the Same that Lieut. Hood gave an account of (it is nearly covd. with Snow). . . . towards evening we met Several Indians in a canoe who were going up the River. they Signed to us that in two Sleeps we Should See the Ocean vessels and white people &c. &c. the Country lower and not So mountanous the River more handsome. . . .

Part 6

The Columbia River to the Pacific Ocean

one of the Columbia River Gorge
waterfalls

Today brought us the promise that we would finally escape the desert and cross the Cascade Mountains. Mount Hood, which stands like a sentinel guarding the Columbia River Gorge, receded to the east, and we could look forward to the ocean.

Since Todd and I were not riding, we had a leisurely morning. I rode out and got watermelon, cantaloupe, peaches and apricots from a fresh produce stand near the campground, and we had a fruit feast for breakfast. After everyone was finished eating and showering, Melina and I rode over to get another peach. She got to ride in my rear pack and held on around my waist.

Our ride in the Rig to Portland was interesting because we could see a clear division between the trees and the desert. The change of environment is accompanied by brisk winds that are channeled through the Columbia River Gorge. This natural wind tunnel makes the area a worldwide mecca for expert wind surfers, vast numbers of which can be seen with their colorful sails cutting across the choppy surface of the Columbia and executing difficult stunts. We drove through White Salmon, a town that looked like it was in the Swiss Alps, and we took a detour to the Oregon side of the River to see some of the waterfalls.

The drive was tough because the strong winds kept pushing the high profile RV across the road. Likewise, the drive in Portland was nerve-racking. Such a large behemoth is tricky to drive in the city.

Our original campground was full, so we ended up in a very disappointing one that was way outside of Portland. This forced us to take a bus in and out of the city. Portland was a change of pace for all of us, but we are looking ahead to being near the ocean.

We wasted no time in heading out of our Portland RV park. Breakfast was in Elmer's Restaurant after which a ride in the Rig took Todd and me up Route 30 to Warren, Oregon where the road ceased to be a divided highway. At this point we got on our bikes and began riding.

What a great ride! The weather was cool, it was sunny, and there was very little headwind. Once more surrounded by trees, our ride took us through Rainier, Oregon and across a bridge where we had to walk our bikes because of close, heavy traffic. From there we traveled on Route 4 to Skamokawa, Washington. Before we reached our camp at Skamokawa (ska-mock-away) State Park, we rode through a town called Cathlemet. It is a picturesque, riverside community that reminds me of a Maine coastal town. We stopped at a place called The Creamery for ice cream. It was a very eclectic store with an ice cream bar, baby toys, religious books and candy. They had a great and unusual variety of ice cream flavors. Todd got an espresso fudge shake, and I tried a licorice shake. The licorice ice cream looked like asphalt, and the shake looked like used oil, but it was, without a doubt, the best shake that I've ever had! All the shakes are served with whipped cream on top and chocolate syrup drizzled over the whipped cream. Unfortunately, the store was for sale.

From Cathlemet it was a short, seven mile ride to Skamokawa State Park where Chris Hawke, a friend that Kris had from her childhood, and his family were waiting for us at the Rig. It was fun to see him, his wife Charlmange and his two boys. They stayed for barbecued burgers and hot dogs, and then they treated us to ice cream at . . . The Creamery. A bit too much ice cream for one day, but it was sooo good! Butter brickle and peppermint ice cream in a large sugar cone!

When we got back to the park, Melina and I went to the beach. We drew pictures in the sand including an eighty-four-foot-square game of tic-tac-toe, and we slid down the sand dunes. We also watched the large ships which passed along the channel very close to shore on their way to the Pacific. Tomorrow we see the Pacific Ocean!

SUNDAY, JULY 31, 1994

Today was the day we've all been anticipating for some time . . . the day we see the ocean. Although our journey does not compare with the magnitude and gravity of the Lewis and Clark expedition, it does give one a better sense of what they might have been feeling.

It doesn't get much smaller than this!

We rode out of Skamokawa camp at about 10:00 A.M.., and traveled fifty-four miles to Fort Canby State Park on the Pacific Ocean. Most of our trip was over rolling hills with gorgeous scenery. One particularly good riding section was a four mile downhill that rewarded us for a previous three mile climb.

Todd and I met up with the Rig at the junction of Routes 4 and 401. We got something to eat and drink and moved on. We rolled through a number of small towns today that again reminded me much of coastal Maine. One sign read: "Entering and Leaving Rosburg."

This environment appeals to me a great deal . . . wonderful tall evergreens, rugged coastline, sand beaches, the Columbia River, etc.

As we rounded the corner by the bridge to Astoria, Oregon, we spotted the Pacific for the first time. At 12:30 P.M. we were in sight of the open ocean, and, needless to say, we were excited and inspired to peddle the remaining fifteen miles to the park. We were almost there and could smell the salt air. At one point, we rode through a tunnel where we pushed a button to reduce the speed limit while we were inside. As we approached Fort Canby State Park, we peddled around a curve in the road and were rewarded with a magnificent view of the ocean waves breaking on the beach. The only thing left to do was find the Rig which

*Gordon and Melina at the
Pacific Ocean*

was a little more difficult than it had been in the past. Fort Canby State Park is a popular spot.

Very soon after arriving at the RV, we all took a walk down to the beach and the ocean. Kris took a picture of me wading into the Pacific, which was such a welcome sight and a much anticipated experience. I must admit that sitting on the beach was a very meaningful, spiritually charged time for me. Dinner was at the Rig, after which we all went to the beach again to take group pictures and watch the numerous kites flying in the Pacific wind. Melina and I went beach exploring as well.

We are all in excellent spirits and are looking forward to our last two days of our journey.

William Clark – November 7th Thursday 1805

Great joy in camp we are in view of the Ocian, this great Pacific Octean which we been so long anxious to See. and the roreing or noise made by the waves brakeing on the rockey Shores (as I suppose) may be heard disti[n]ctly

Monday, August 1, 1994

After waking at 6:00 A.M., I went for a thirty-minute run on the beach. Today was a light day of riding, and I love to run by the ocean. When everyone was ready to go, we set out for the Fort Canby Interpretive Center but found it to be closed. It was 9:00 A.M., and it did not open until 10:00 A.M. We all drove in the Rig to Astoria, Oregon, a ten-minute ride across the narrow, three-mile Astoria Bridge, and had breakfast in a place called the Pig 'N Pancake. I had a huge breakfast because it was the last day that I would be active enough to burn an enormous number of calories.

Fort Clatsop, a replica of the Lewis and Clark expedition's winter quarters of 1805–1806, was our next stop, and, as it was only a few miles from Astoria, we all rode in the Rig.

The staff at the fort were very interested in our adventure.

We saw a demonstration of early 19th century rifle loading at the fort, and we visited the exact site where Lewis and Clark paddled ashore in their boats. Kris took pictures of Todd and me pretending to paddle one of the dugout canoes, as we sat inside one of them.

We also watched a wonderful movie at the visitors center about Lewis and Clark that we ended up purchasing.

Todd and I began our final ride from the fort and headed for our last riding destination, Cannon Beach, Oregon. Following Route 101 South was an easy ride. We stopped in Seaside, Oregon at 12:30 P.M. to meet Gene Miles, the city manager, and to visit the bronze statue of Lewis and Clark on the promenade, which marks the end of the trail for the expedition's permanent party.

We looked over the Californiaesque beach and saw Tillamook Head, which was on tomorrow's hiking agenda.

A visit to the Salt Works, where three of Lewis and Clark's men had boiled sea water in order to make salt for the party, was interesting to see.

There's a brass plaque, which may not photograph well that reads:

"Lewis and Clark Salt Cairn on January 2, 1806. The Salt Works was established by the three "salt makers" of the Lewis and Clark expedition Joseph Fields, William Brackman and George Gibson who remained here until February 20, 1806. These men, assisted at times by hunters and packers, were able during this period to tediously extract approximately four bushels of salt by boiling sea water day and night in five metal "kittles." The expedition had run out of salt before arrival at their winter camp at Fort Clatsop ten miles to the northeast, and it was very necessary for curing meat and preparing for the return trip to civilization. This actual site was established by a committee of the Oregon Historical Society in 1900 upon the testimony of Jenny Michel of Seaside whose Clatsop Indian father remembered seeing the white men boiling water and pointed out this place to her when she was a young girl. She was born in this vicinity about 1816 and died in 1905. This plaque was erected by the Seaside Lions Club in 1965.

Fort Clatsop

Melina and Gordon in a Fort Clatsop bunk

Todd and Gordon "paddling" at Fort Clatsop

Lewis and Clark statue at Seaside, Oregon

The Salt Works

view of Tillamook Head from Seaside Beach

After taking some additional photographs, we set out for Cannon Beach, which was only seven miles further down Route 101. We were psyched about being close to the end of our riding, and I was looking forward to getting off this bike and hanging the sucker up. The fates, however, couldn't resist throwing one more hill in our way, but it was negotiated pretty easily. Our arrival at Cannon Beach was at 4:22 P.M., having done 24.89 miles. Kris waved us into the RV park drive, and Melina presented Todd and me with one dozen roses – one rose for each of us per week on the trail. I appreciate Kris and Susie's efforts more than I can say.

We were officially done with our Bianchi bicycles, which served us very well, and we celebrated by looking around the town of Cannon Beach and going out to dinner at a seafood restaurant called Doogers Seafood Grill. We were all happy to be at the end of the trail and looked forward to our final hike tomorrow, which should be awesome.

Recalling the events and adventures that led up to this point, it is evident how our thoughts and actions affect others. If we approach our daily lives carefully, attentively and with awareness, we can begin to link events in our lives. Even events that seem meaningless have a purpose. Normally, when we find a significant and unexpected or accidental correlation between two or more events or ideas, we call it a coincidence, but perhaps there are no coincidences or accidents. Perhaps every occurrence, however insignificant it might seem in our eyes, is intertwined and related to others and has an important purpose. To be sure, our minds are too simple to process the entire complexity of life's spider web of events, but thinking about the implications of this possibility allows for a wonderful sense of freedom, security and responsibility. Adopting this understanding allows us to see ourselves and our actions in a new light. Everything we do is tied in some way to everything else. Every action and thought has been prompted by an earlier action and/or thought, and each present moment will have a very definite effect upon the future. No longer are there insignificant acts. There are no coincidences. Every event is a brick in the continuing structure of life, every action a necessary piece of the puzzle and every one of us a hero.

The human race is a small part of the world around us, forever linked to the condition of the earth as a whole. We all must monitor our actions carefully and remember that there are no insignificant thoughts or acts, for each has its purpose and will touch or spark those yet to come. A human being as a body is very small in comparison to the earth and the heavens, but the result of what an individual does can be monumental and far-reaching, indeed.

Gordon T. Ward

MERIWETHER LEWIS – SUNDAY AUGUST 18TH 1805.

[written six days after he crossed the Continental Divide]

This day I completed my thirty first year, and conceived that I had in all human probability now existed about half the period which I am to remain in this Sublunary world. I reflected that I had as yet done but little, very little, indeed, to further the hapiness of the human race or to advance the information of the succeeding generation. I viewed with regret the many hours I have spent in indolence, and now soarly feel the want of that information which those hours would have given me had they been judiciously expended. but since they are past and cannot be recalled, I dash from me the gloomy thought, and resolved in future, to redouble my exertions and at last indeavour to promote those two primary objects of human existence, by giving them the aid of that portion of talents which nature and fortune have bestoed on me; or in future, to live for mankind, as I have heretofore lived for myself.

TUESDAY, AUGUST 2, 1994

Today included a six-mile hike over Tillamook Head between Seaside and Ecola State Park.

It was the trail taken by William Clark, Sacagawea and a few other men to purchase whale oil from a local group of Native Americans and to view a beached whale that the tribe was rendering.

Kris drove us back to Seaside, and Todd, Susie and I began our final leg of our journey. We were passed by a man at the trailhead that was running his dogs up the road and into the trail. The first two miles were very steep with lots of switchbacks. The Northwest Pacific rain forest environment was cool, damp, lush and extraordinary with enormous trees, grotesquely shaped branches and thick green moss that hung from everything.

I was fascinated by the area and took many photographs. The lookouts did not reveal much of a view because of the rain clouds and fog that hung over the area and cloaked the beach below us. I photographed a downed tree that I determined to be approximately 174 years old by counting its annular rings. The tree was about twenty inches in diameter, and I hung my watch on the surface for a comparison reference. After doing this, I placed my watch on one of the huge, six-foot diameter trees for another photograph and imagined how much older the large hemlocks were – perhaps 450 years old or more! It was interesting to think about the fact that we were surrounded by living things that were here when William Clark had passed through the area, especially at an area called Clark's View, a spectacular overlook.

We were passed by the man with the dogs, and we in turn passed him at an overlook spot. One of his dogs bared his teeth at us, and the man put him back on a leash. He had a Boston Bull Terrier and a very protective French Bull Terrier. The man himself was dressed only in shorts and hiking boots and did not want to converse with us. All in all, he presented himself as a very unusual character.

As we proceeded on over Tillamook Head and down to Indian Beach at Ecola State Park, the sun came out, and we were presented with some spectacular sights. We took many photos, with some overlooking our final destination.

The fact that the sun appeared at the end of our trip seemed meaningful to me as if our guardian angels were somehow rewarding our efforts of the past six weeks. Although I was stung by a bee on the last few hundred yards of the trail, it did not dampen the excitement

I was feeling at completing our journey. We headed down the last descent in the trail with Haystack Rock in our sights and Cannon Beach stretching out into the distance. The trip was completed as we stepped into the beach parking lot. It was strange to realize that we were finished, yet there was no one to acknowledge this fact. We did not expect anything, but it seemed queer to end a six-week trip and fourteen months of planning in such a calm, nonchalant manner. Inside, I could not quite find the words to express my bittersweet feelings, but the look in each other's eyes said it all. I thought of a poem that I wrote in 1991 because, for me, it summed up the changes in my feelings, thoughts, experiences and outlook.

enormous trees along the Tillamook Head Trail   *Clark's View Overlook*

Cannon Beach and the end of our journey

John's Brook

I first asked the people:
      "How do you see the world
Through eyes so darkly veiled
That they are trained to focus
On only brilliant images
To occupy your sheltered lives?"

And one did answer:
      "I focus not on petty things
But on the charged, electric life
That flings my eyes wide open
And fills my senses with panoramic sights,
Much more than I can comprehend,

Extended mountains of impulses
For which I must search and wait."
I then asked the children:
      "How do you see the world
Through eyes so alert
That all within your scope
Demands your time,
If only for a fleeting second?"

And one child did answer:
      "I see the wonder in miniature,
The world anew in a microcosm.
I do not tarry long

Or contemplate much of what I see.
It is as if I crawled across a sun-filled
      cathedral window
Ecstatically hopping from color to color
But denied the comprehension of the image."

I then looked inward and asked myself:
      "How could I best see the world
Through eyes so numbed by time
That I have lost my way
And fail to see the well marked trail
Toward my own horizon?"
And my spirit replied . . . in a whisper:

"You must see the world both small
      and large
With eyes as wondrous as a child's,
Eyes that see the pebbles on the mountain,
The needles on the forest floor,
And the colors of the morning.
But blend this with the eye of age
Whose gift it is to comprehend
The jagged range of mountains,
The soul of the people,
And the image in the window."

Lewis and Clark

Todd and Gordon

About the Author

Gordon T. Ward was born in Tacoma, Washington, and his family moved to New Jersey when he was eleven months old. Both of his parents were talented artists and enjoyed the outdoors, and his family divided their time between the family's home in Bernardsville, New Jersey and a summer cottage in Maine. After high school, Gordon went on to major in fine arts and psychology at Fairleigh Dickinson University in Madison, New Jersey, where his father was a professor. Gordon soon began his own career in education, teaching language arts and history. In the summer of 1994, he used his love of history and the outdoors to cycle, hike and canoe 1,800 miles of the Lewis and Clark Trail in order to establish a school scholarship.

A lifelong writer, Gordon used his experiences on the Lewis and Clark Trail to write *Life on the Shoulder,* which details his experiences and the changes that have taken place in the varied environments along the trail. The author has also written speeches, articles, a self-published collection of original poetry, and completed a manuscript entitled "A Bit of

Earth" about the history of the land where he spent his childhood. It includes personal anecdotes and addresses his belief in the link that we all have to the past and the future. Gordon also manages his own, part-time, experiential education company, GTW SERVICES LLC, which allows him to offer teambuilding programs to many types of groups and deliver presentations on various topics.

The author currently resides in Bedminster, New Jersey. Gordon loves being a father to his daughter and son, and continually pursues his passions for songwriting, playing guitar, and running.